SUMMER EXPRESS

GRADES 2&3

NEW YORK • TORONTO • LONDON • AUCKLAND • SYDNEY
MEXICO CITY • NEW DELHI • HONG KONG • BUENOS AIRES

Cover design by Brian LaRossa
Cover photo by Ariel Skelley/Corbis
Interior illustrations by Robert Alley, Abbey Carter, Maxie Chambliss, Sue Dennen,
Shelley Dieterichs, Jane Dippold, Julie Durrell, Rusty Fletcher, James Hale,
Mike Moran, Sherry Neidigh, Cary Pillo, Carol Tiernon, and Lynn Vineyard

ISBN-13 978-0-545-22692-9 / ISBN-10 0-545-22692-9
Copyright © 2010 by Scholastic Inc. All rights reserved. Printed in the U.S.A.

12 13 14 15 16 17 18 19 20   08   20 19 18 17 16 15 14

Table of Contents

Dear Parent Letter 4

Terrific Tips for Using This Book 6

Week 1 9

Week 2 21

Week 3 33

Week 4 45

Week 5 57

Week 6 69

Week 7 81

Week 8 93

Week 9 105

Week 10 117

Answer Key 129

Certificate 143

Stickers . . . . Insert

Dear Parent:

Congratulations! You hold in your hands an exceptional educational tool that will give your child a head start into the coming school year.

Inside this book, you'll find one hundred practice pages that will help your child review and learn reading and writing skills, grammar, addition and subtraction, and so much more! *Summer Express* is divided into 10 weeks, with two practice pages for each day of the week, Monday to Friday. However, feel free to use the pages in any order that your child would like. Here are other features you'll find inside:

- A weekly **incentive chart** and **certificate** to motivate and reward your child for his or her efforts.

- A sheet of **colorful stickers**. There are small stickers for completing the activities each day, as well as a large sticker to use as a weekly reward.

- Suggestions for fun, creative **learning activities** you can do with your child each week.

- A **recommended reading list** of age-appropriate books that you and your child can read throughout the summer.

- A **certificate of completion** to celebrate your child's accomplishments.

We hope you and your child will have a lot of fun as you work together to complete this workbook.

Enjoy!
The editors

Terrific Tips for Using This Book

1 Pick a good time for your child to work on the activities. You may want to do it around mid-morning after play, or early afternoon when your child is not too tired.

2 Make sure your child has all the supplies he or she needs, such as pencils and crayons. Set aside a special place for your child to work.

3 At the beginning of each week, discuss with your child how many minutes a day he or she would like to read. Write the goal at the top of the incentive chart for the week. (We recommend reading 15 to 20 minutes a day with your child who is entering 3rd grade.)

4 Reward your child's efforts with the small stickers at the end of each day. As an added bonus, let your child affix a large sticker at the bottom of the incentive chart for completing the activities each week.

5 Encourage your child to complete the worksheet, but don't force the issue. While you may want to ensure that your child succeeds, it's also important that your child maintain a positive and relaxed attitude toward school and learning.

6 After you've given your child a few minutes to look over the practice pages he or she will be working on, ask your child to tell you his or her plan of action: "Tell me about what we're doing on these pages." Hearing the explanation aloud can provide you with insights into your child's thinking processes. Can he or she complete the work independently? With guidance? If your child needs support, try offering a choice about which family member might help. Giving your child a choice can help boost confidence and help him or her feel more ownership of the work to be done.

7 When your child has finished the workbook, present him or her with the certificate of completion on page 143. Feel free to frame or laminate the certificate and display it on the wall for everyone to see. Your child will be so proud!

Skill-Building Activities for Any Time

The following activities are designed to complement the ten weeks of practice pages in this book. These activities don't take more than a few minutes to complete and are just a handful of ways in which you can enrich and enliven your child's learning. Use the activities to take advantage of the time you might ordinarily disregard—for example, standing in line or waiting at a bus stop. You'll be working to practice key skills and have fun together at the same time.

Finding Real-Life Connections

One of the reasons for schooling is to help children function out in the real world, to empower them with the abilities they'll truly need. So why not put those developing skills into action by enlisting your child's help with creating a grocery list, reading street signs, sorting pocket change, and so on? He or she can apply reading, writing, science, and math skills in important and practical ways, connecting what he or she is learning with everyday tasks.

An Eye for Patterns

A red-brick sidewalk, a beaded necklace, a Sunday newspaper—all show evidence of structure and organization. You can help your child recognize something's structure or organization by observing and talking about patterns they see. Your child will apply his or her developing ability to spot patterns across all school subject areas, including alphabet letter formation (writing), attributes of shapes and solids (geometry), and characteristics of narrative stories (reading). Being able to notice patterns is a skill shared by effective readers and writers, scientists, and mathematicians.

Journals as Learning Tools

Most of us associate journal writing with reading comprehension, but having your child keep a journal can help you keep up with his or her developing skills in other academic areas as well—from telling time to matching rhymes. To get started, provide your child with several sheets of paper, folded in half, and stapled together. Explain that he or she will be writing and/or drawing in the journal to complement the practice pages completed each week. Encourage your child to draw or write about what he or she found easy, what was difficult, or what was fun. Before moving on to another set of practice pages, take a few minutes to read and discuss that week's journal entries together.

Promote Reading at Home

◆ Let your child catch you in the act of reading for pleasure, whether you like reading science fiction novels or do-it-yourself magazines. Store them someplace that encourages you to read in front of your child and **demonstrate that reading is an activity you enjoy**. For example, locate your reading materials on the coffee table instead of your nightstand.

◆ Set aside a family reading time. By designating a reading time each week, your family is assured an opportunity to discuss with each other what you're reading. You can, for example, share a funny quote from an article. Or, your child can tell you his or her favorite part of a story. The key is to **make a family tradition of reading and sharing books** of all kinds together.

◆ **Put together collections of reading materials** your child can access easily. Gather them in baskets or bins that you can place in the family room, the car, and your child's bedroom. You can refresh your child's library by borrowing materials from your community's library, buying used books, or swapping books and magazines with friends and neighbors.

Skills Review and Practice

Educators have established learning standards for math and language arts. Listed below are some of the important skills covered in *Summer Express* that will help your child review and prepare for the coming school year so that he or she is better prepared to meet these learning standards.

Math

Skills Your Child Will Review

- identifying simple fractions
- adding and subtracting 1- and 2-digit numbers with regrouping
- identifying place value
- telling time
- identifying coins and their values
- identifying shapes
- using simple equations

Skills Your Child Will Practice to Prepare for Grade Three

- matching number words with numerals
- adding 3-digit numbers with regrouping
- subtracting 2-digit numbers without regrouping
- subtracting simple fractions with common denominators
- multiplying (e.g., addition sentences, arrays)
- division with remainders
- measuring weight (e.g., ounces and pounds)
- identifying geometric solids
- matching familiar items with geometric solids
- using a bar graph to record coin values and their equivalents

Language Arts

Skills Your Child Will Review

- using descriptive words to clarify meaning
- using sentence variety (e.g., statements, exclamations, commands)
- identifying main idea, sequence of events, main characters, causes and effects
- making inferences, drawing conclusions, comparing and contrasting
- reading for supporting details
- identifying real or fantasy within the context of story

Skills Your Child Will Practice to Prepare for Grade Three

- proofreading (e.g., meaning, spelling, sentence variety, and grammar)
- expanding and combining sentences
- using parts of speech (e.g., common nouns, proper nouns, plural nouns, pronouns, present- and past-tense verbs, adjectives, prepositions)
- punctuating (e.g., possessives, quotation marks, contractions)
- writing in upper- and lowercase cursive letters
- writing cursive numerals 0–9
- demonstrating knowledge of level-appropriate reading vocabulary (e.g., homophones, synonyms, antonyms, prefixes [un-], compound words, analogies, word relationships)

Helping Your Child Get Ready: Week 1

These are the skills your child will be working on this week.

Math
- adding 1- and 2-digit numbers with regrouping
- subtracting 2-digit numbers without regrouping

Reading
- classifying
- sequencing

Writing
- sentence punctuation
- proofreading

Vocabulary
- examining similarities
- sight words

Grammar
- compound nouns

Here are some activities you and your child might enjoy.

Sizzling Synonyms! The first time your child says, "It's hot outside," challenge him or her to come up with as many words as possible that mean the same thing as *hot*. You can try this with other weather words such as *rainy* or *cloudy*.

Summer Goal Suggest that your child come up with a plan to achieve a goal by the end of the summer. For example, he or she may wish to become an expert on a favorite animal or learn to count in another language. Help him or her map out a way to be successful. Periodically, check to see how your child is progressing.

Order, Order! Play a ranking game. Choose three related items and ask your child to put them in order. Ask him or her to explain the choice. For example, if you chose ice cube, snow ball, and frozen lake, your child might say small, medium, and large; or cold, colder, coldest.

Sun Safety Talk about sun safety with your child. Ask him or her to write a list of ways to stay safe in the sun. Post it in a prominent place!

Your child might enjoy reading the following books:

Bringing the Rain to Kapiti Plain
by Verna Aardema

The New Kid on the Block
by Jack Prelutsky

Coming to America:
The Story of Immigration
by Betsy Maestro

_____

's Incentive Chart: Week 1

This week, I plan to read _____ minutes each day.

CHART YOUR PROGRESS HERE.

Week 1	Day 1	Day 2	Day 3	Day 4	Day 5
I read for...	minutes	minutes	minutes	minutes	minutes
Put a sticker to show you completed each day's work.					

Congratulations!

Wow! You did a great job this week!

Place sticker here.

Parent or Caregiver's Signature _____

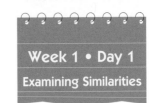
Things We Use

People use different tools to do things. Read the list.

Draw a line from each player to the things for that sport.

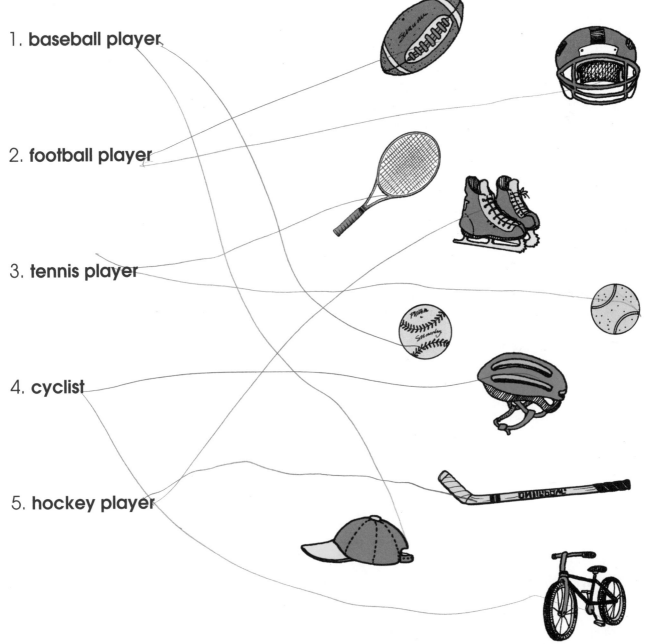

1. **baseball player**

2. **football player**

3. **tennis player**

4. **cyclist**

5. **hockey player**

Talk with someone about how each item is used.

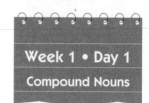
Adding Words

A **compound noun** is made up of two smaller words put together.

cup + **cake** = **cupcake**

Can you figure out what these compound nouns are?
Read the clues. Then write the compound noun.

1. A **cloth** that covers a **table** is a _tablecloth_

2. **Corn** that goes **pop** is _popcorn_

3. A **book** for a **cook** is a _cookbook_

4. An **apple** made into **sauce** is _applesauce_

5. A **cake** with **fruit** in it is a _fruit cake_

6. **Meat** made into a **ball** is a _meat ball_

7. A **melon** with lots of **water** in it is a _watermelon_

8. A **berry** that is **blue** is a _blueberry_

Write a menu for a meal you would like. Use some compound nouns in your menu.

Scholastic Inc. *Summer Express: Between Grades 2 & 3*

Kaleidoscope

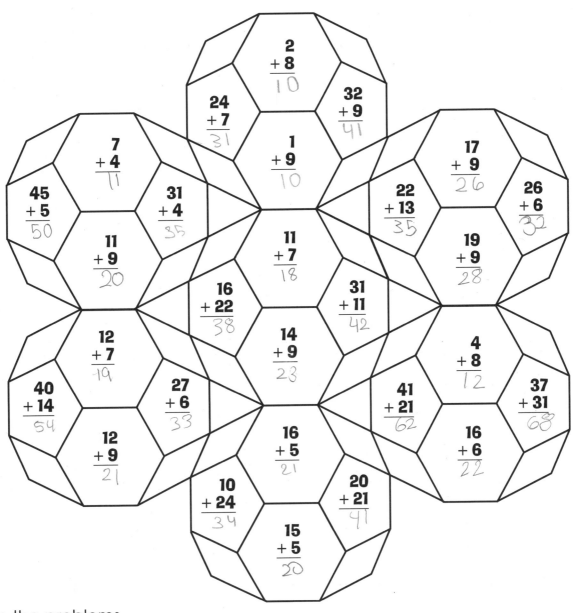

$$\begin{array}{r} 2 \\ + 8 \\ \hline 10 \end{array}$$

$$\begin{array}{r} 24 \\ + 7 \\ \hline 31 \end{array}$$

$$\begin{array}{r} 32 \\ + 9 \\ \hline 41 \end{array}$$

$$\begin{array}{r} 1 \\ + 9 \\ \hline 10 \end{array}$$

$$\begin{array}{r} 7 \\ + 4 \\ \hline 11 \end{array}$$

$$\begin{array}{r} 17 \\ + 9 \\ \hline 26 \end{array}$$

$$\begin{array}{r} 45 \\ + 5 \\ \hline 50 \end{array}$$

$$\begin{array}{r} 31 \\ + 4 \\ \hline 35 \end{array}$$

$$\begin{array}{r} 22 \\ + 13 \\ \hline 35 \end{array}$$

$$\begin{array}{r} 26 \\ + 6 \\ \hline 32 \end{array}$$

$$\begin{array}{r} 11 \\ + 9 \\ \hline 20 \end{array}$$

$$\begin{array}{r} 11 \\ + 7 \\ \hline 18 \end{array}$$

$$\begin{array}{r} 19 \\ + 9 \\ \hline 28 \end{array}$$

$$\begin{array}{r} 16 \\ + 22 \\ \hline 38 \end{array}$$

$$\begin{array}{r} 31 \\ + 11 \\ \hline 42 \end{array}$$

$$\begin{array}{r} 12 \\ + 7 \\ \hline 19 \end{array}$$

$$\begin{array}{r} 14 \\ + 9 \\ \hline 23 \end{array}$$

$$\begin{array}{r} 4 \\ + 8 \\ \hline 12 \end{array}$$

$$\begin{array}{r} 40 \\ + 14 \\ \hline 54 \end{array}$$

$$\begin{array}{r} 27 \\ + 6 \\ \hline 33 \end{array}$$

$$\begin{array}{r} 41 \\ + 21 \\ \hline 62 \end{array}$$

$$\begin{array}{r} 37 \\ + 31 \\ \hline 68 \end{array}$$

$$\begin{array}{r} 12 \\ + 9 \\ \hline 21 \end{array}$$

$$\begin{array}{r} 16 \\ + 5 \\ \hline 21 \end{array}$$

$$\begin{array}{r} 16 \\ + 6 \\ \hline 22 \end{array}$$

$$\begin{array}{r} 10 \\ + 24 \\ \hline 34 \end{array}$$

$$\begin{array}{r} 20 \\ + 21 \\ \hline 41 \end{array}$$

$$\begin{array}{r} 15 \\ + 5 \\ \hline 20 \end{array}$$

Solve the problems.

If the answer is between 1 and 30, color the shape yellow.

If the answer is between 31 and 99, color the shape gray.

Finish by coloring the other shapes with the colors of your choice.

Extra: Name two numbers that when added together equal 27.

21 + 6 = 27

Scholastic Inc.   Summer Express: Between Grades 2 & 3

Sunny Sentences

*Every sentence begins with a **capital letter**.*
*A **telling sentence** ends with a **period** (.).*
*An **asking sentence** ends with a **question mark** (?).*

Rewrite each sentence correctly.

1. the sun is the closest star to Earth

   <u>The Sun is the closest to Earth.</u>

2. the sun is not the brightest star

   <u>The Sun is not brightest Star.</u>

3. what is the temperature of the sun

   <u>What is the temperature of the Sun?</u>

4. the sun is a ball of hot gas

   _____

5. how large is the sun

   _____

6. will the sun ever burn out

   _____

Scholastic Inc. *Summer Express: Between Grades 2 & 3*

Which One Doesn't Belong?

 Look for similarities when grouping items.

Read each list. Cross out the word that doesn't belong. Then choose a word from the kite that belongs with each list and write it in the blank.

1. grouchy   mad   ~~cheerful~~   fussy   _angry_

2. north   ~~away~~   east   south   _west_

3. ~~goat~~   blue jay   robin   eagle   _parakeet_

4. juice   milk   tea   ~~mud~~   _lemonade_

5. hand   ~~toe~~   foot   head   _arm_

6. David   Bob   Ronald   ~~Sarah~~   _George_

7. ~~spinach~~   cake   cookies   pie   _Pudding_

8. glue   ~~bicycle~~   pencils   scissors   _Crayons_

9. penny   nickel   quarter   ~~marble~~   _dime_

On the kite:
arm
~~dime~~
~~George~~
~~pudding~~
~~lemonade~~
~~parakeet~~
~~crayons~~
~~angry~~
~~west~~

Now read these categories. In each box, write the number from the above list that matches the category.

Birds 3	Desserts 7	Sour Feelings 1
Boys' Names 6	Money 9	School Supplies 8
Directions 2	Body Parts 5	Drinks 4

 Write a list of five things that go with this category: Things That Are Hot.

Sun   fire   lava   magma   Venus

A Happy Camper

➤ *Complete:*
Every sentence begins with a _____ .
A statement ends with a _____ .
A question ends with a _____ .

Uh oh! Dalton was in a hurry when he wrote this letter. Help him find 10 mistakes. Circle them.

Dear Mom and Dad,

camp is so cool? today we went swimming? do you know what the best part of camp is. i think fishing is my favorite thing to do. did you feed my hamster. I really miss you?

Love, Dalton

Now choose two questions and two statements from Dalton's letter. Rewrite each correctly.

1. _____

2. _____

3. _____

4. _____

 On another sheet of paper, write a letter to a friend or family member. Include two statements and two questions.

Scholastic Inc. *Summer Express: Between Grades 2 & 3*

Super Star

Solve the problems. If the answer is between 1 and 20, color the shape yellow. If the answer is between 21 and 40, color the shape white. If the answer is between 41 and 90, color the shape blue.

 Write five subtraction problems that have answers between 10 and 20.

 17

Hello, Island!

About 30 years ago, some fishermen were on their boat near Iceland. Suddenly they saw smoke coming from the sea. Then the top of a volcano rose out of the water. Soon red-hot rock began to pour down its sides. It looked like the sea was on fire. At last the volcano cooled down. It became a new island. People named the island Surtsey.

Read how the island of Surtsey was made. Show the correct order of what happened. Write the numbers from 1–4 on the lines.

____ **Red-hot rock poured down its sides.**

____ **Smoke came out of the sea.**

____ **The new island was named Surtsey.**

____ **The volcano cooled down.**

Fill in the circles in order. Use the numbers and sentences above to help you. The first one is done for you.

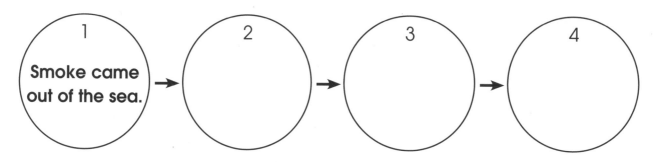

1
Smoke came out of the sea. → 2 → 3 → 4

 Tell someone how Surtsey became an island. Draw pictures to show what happened.

Scholastic Inc.   Summer Express: Between Grades 2 & 3

Turn on the Lights

Lighthouses warn ships that are near land. The first lighthouses were fires. People would build the fires on hilltops along the coast. Later people built towers. The light from their candles could be seen from far away. Then oil lamps were used. Today electricity runs a lighthouse's powerful lamps.

lamp

tower

Read how lighthouses changed.

Show the correct order of what happened. Write the numbers from 1–4 on the lines.

____ **Oil lamps lit lighthouses.**

____ **Lighthouses use electric light.**

____ **Fires were built on hillsides.**

____ **Candles were used.**

Fill in the circles in order. Use the numbers and sentences above to help you.

1 → 2 → 3 → 4

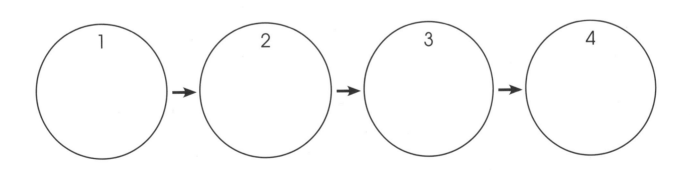

MORE! **Read *The Little Red Lighthouse* and the *Great Gray Bridge* by Hildegarde Swift.**

Find the Word

Complete the sentences below with words from the Word Box. Then find the words in the puzzle. Words may go across, down, or diagonally. We did the first one for you.

1. I chose a pumpkin that had no bumps and was perfectly __round__.

2. Sarah had a question about her homework, so she picked up the phone to _____ Tanisha.

3. After Juan ate the hot fudge sundae, his stomach felt very _____.

4. When my mom went _____ on a trip, she sent me postcards.

5. Miko's cat likes to sit _____ her lap while Miko reads.

6. Sam had to _____ on his dog's leash to keep him away from the hornet's nest.

A	R	H	L	U	I
D	W	L	U	P	P
I	A	A	D	O	U
C	E	F	Y	N	L
R	O	U	N	D	L
P	U	F	U	L	L

Word Box

away	~~round~~
pull	full
call	upon

Scholastic Inc.   Summer Express: Between Grades 2 & 3

Helping Your Child Get Ready: Week 2

These are the skills your child will be working on this week.

Math
- subtracting 2-digit numbers with regrouping
- adding 3-digit numbers with regrouping

Reading
- making inferences
- comprehension

Writing
- adjectives
- sentence punctuation

Vocabulary
- rhyming words
- part/whole analogies

Grammar
- subject/verb agreement
- present tense

Handwriting
- uppercase cursive letters

Here are some activities you and your child might enjoy.

Scrambled Summer Have your child write the words *summer vacation* on a sheet of paper and cut apart the letters. Encourage your child to use the letters to make new words. For variety, your child might also use the names of animals such as elephant, alligator, or hippopotamus.

Terrific Timelines Help your child practice sequencing by creating timelines. For example, he or she can create a timeline of the daily routine. Encourage him or her to write sentences to describe what happens first, next, and so on. Challenge your child to create a timeline that includes the week's events, or one that shows at least one important event that occurred in each year of your child's life.

Rhyme Relay Pick a word, such as *cat* or *dog*, to begin a rhyme relay. Take turns with your child saying words that rhyme with it.

Newspaper Scavenger Hunt You can use a newspaper for many different scavenger hunts. For example, ask your child to find a certain number of proper nouns, adjectives, quotation marks, or exclamation points. Or, you may wish to challenge your child to find different parts of a newspaper, such as headlines, political cartoons, or captions.

Your child might enjoy reading the following books:

Black Cat
by Christopher Meyers

Dr. De Soto
by William Steig

Knots on a Counting Rope
by John Archambault

_____ **'s Incentive Chart: Week 2**

Name Here

This week, I plan to read _____ minutes each day.

CHART YOUR PROGRESS HERE.

Week 2 I read for...	Day 1	Day 2	Day 3	Day 4	Day 5
	minutes	minutes	minutes	minutes	minutes
Put a sticker to show you completed each day's work.					

Congratulations!

Wow! You did a great job this week!

#1

Place sticker here.

Parent or Caregiver's Signature _____

a-z

A B C D E F
G H I J K L M
N O P Q R S T
U V W X Y Z

Write.

Figure It Out

Read each sentence. Then color the numbered space in the picture that matches the number of the correct answer.

He rode his bike.
Who rode it?
1. a boy
2. a girl

Please bait my hook.
What am I doing?
7. fishing
8. playing baseball

Sorry! I broke it.
What could it be?
13. a stuffed animal
14. a crystal vase

Look at the dark cloud.
Where should you look?
19. down
20. up

The lamb lost its mother.
Who is its mother?
21. a sheep
22. a horse

She wore a red hat.
Who wore it?
23. a man
24. a woman

I see a thousand stars.
What time is it?
25. noon
26. night

Let's throw snowballs!
What time of year is it?
3. summer
4. winter

Breakfast is ready!
What time is it?
9. night
10. morning

He's a professor.
What is he?
15. an adult
16. a baby

Run, John, run!
What sport is John in?
5. swimming
6. track

I'm so thirsty.
What will I do?
11. drink something
12. eat something

It won't fit in the car.
What is it?
17. a football
18. a swing set

Riddle: What begins with T, ends with T, and has T in it?
Find it in the puzzle.

Up the Elephant's Trunk

The elephant once said to me,
"Mouse, please climb in my nose
And go until I say to stop,
Then scratch there with your toes."

I climbed inside the long, deep trunk,
The air was damp and gray.
I walked across some peanut shells
And grass and bits of hay.

Then halfway up the bumpy trail
The elephant yelled, "Stop!"
"Scratch!" he said. "With all your might,
Just jump and kick and hop."

I scratched and itched and itched and scratched,
He finally yelled, "Enough!"
And then he blew me out his trunk
With lots of other stuff.

The elephant gave one big laugh
And said, "I thank you much."
And then he put his trunk on me
And gave me a warm touch.

★ SPECIAL WORDS ★

nose   long   trunk   damp   bumpy   trail

Up the Elephant's Trunk

Reading Comprehension

Fill in the blanks with the word that best completes the sentence.

1. The elephant said, "Mouse, please _____ in my nose."

    walk   jump   climb   get

2. I walked across some peanut _____ .

    crumbs   shells   leaves   butter

3. Halfway up the bumpy _____ the elephant yelled, "Stop!"

    road   path   street   trail

4. "Scratch!" he said. "With all your might, just jump and kick and

    _____ ."

    hop   stomp   step   fall

5. He finally _____ , "Enough!"

    said   cried   yelled   shouted

Rhyme Time

Circle the words in each column that rhyme with the word in bold.
What other words rhyme with that word? Write them on the lines below.

nose	**long**	**trunk**	**damp**	**bumpy**	**trail**
not	song	dunk	camp	lumpy	pail
goes	lone	sunk	ramp	humpy	sail
bows	wrong	truck	dump	puppy	tail
_____	_____	_____	_____	_____	_____
_____	_____	_____	_____	_____	_____

Scholastic Inc.   Summer Express: Between Grades 2 & 3

Grandma's Quilt

Solve the problems. If the answer is between 1 and 50, color the shape pink. If the answer is between 51 and 100, color the shape blue. Finish the design by coloring the other shapes with the colors of your choice.

 Amelia bought 30 tickets for rides at the carnival. She used 15 tickets in the first hour. How many tickets did she have left?

 27

How to Agree

If the naming part of a sentence is a noun or pronoun that names one, the verb ends in **-s**, except for the pronouns **I** and **you**. If the naming part is a noun or pronoun that names more than one, the verb does not end in **-s**.

Read each sentence. Circle the correct verb to complete it.

1. John and his family (camp, camps) in the woods.

2. Alice (like, likes) hiking the best.

3. John (walk, walks) ahead of everyone.

4. Mom and John (build, builds) a campfire.

5. Dad and Alice (cook, cooks) dinner over the fire.

6. Alice and Mom (crawl, crawls) into the tent.

Choose two of the verbs you circled. Write a sentence using each verb.

_____

_____

Scholastic Inc.   Summer Express: Between Grades 2 & 3

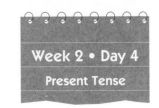
Draw a Picture

Verbs tell when action takes place. Present-tense verbs tell about action that is happening now. A verb showing the action of one person ends in **-s**. A verb telling the action of more than one person does not end in **-s**.

The boy sings.   The boys sing.

In the sentences below, underline each action verb. Then draw a picture that shows the action. Be sure to show if it is one person or animal doing the action or more than one person or animal doing the action.

1. **Four birds sit on the fence.**	2. **That dog digs.**
3. **A man sells hotdogs.**	4. **The girls run.**

Choose one of the pictures you drew. Write a short story about it.

Pick a Part

Circle the correct word to complete each sentence.

1. A leg is a part of a table, and a seat is a part of a _____.
   A. rug   B. chair   C. bed

2. A string is a part of a harp, and a button is a part of a _____.
   A. shirt   B. snap   C. circle

3. A screen is a part of a TV, and a hand is a part of a _____.
   A. broom   B. clock   C. knob

4. A yolk is a part of an egg, and a pit is a part of a _____.
   A. peach   B. hen   C. word

5. A heel is a part of a foot, and an eye is a part of a _____.
   A. toe   B. nose   C. face

6. A stove is a part of a kitchen, and a couch is a part of a _____.
   A. den   B. sink   C. floor

7. A wing is a part of a bird, and a sleeve is a part of a _____.
   A. nest   B. sweater   C. pocket

8. A drawer is a part of a desk, and a pedal is a part of a _____.
   A. ladder   B. step   C. bike

 Name two things that each of these can be a part of: ear, eye, arm, leg, and neck.

Scholastic Inc.   Summer Express: Between Grades 2 & 3

Tricky Twins

Sandy and Mandy are having a twin party. There are six sets of twins, but only one set of identical twins. To find the identical twins, solve the addition problems under each person. The identical twins have the same answer.

207
+ 434

126
+ 89

328
+ 367

257
+ 568

547
+ 129

624
+ 127

108
+ 107

229
+ 337

258
+ 378

379
+ 336

417
+ 109

153
+ 494

Seashore Sentences

Complete:

A _____ ends with a period.

A _____ ends with a question mark.

An _____ ends with an exclamation point.

Write a statement (S), a question (Q), and an exclamation (E) about each picture.

S _____

_____

Q _____

_____

E _____

_____

S _____

_____

Q _____

_____

E _____

_____

 On another sheet of paper, write a statement, a question, and an exclamation about a cartoon in the newspaper.

Scholastic Inc. Summer Express: Between Grades 2 & 3

Helping Your Child Get Ready: Week 3

These are the skills your child will be working on this week.

Math
- simple equations
- adding 3-digit numbers with regrouping

Reading
- comprehension
- reading for details

Writing
- writing to a prompt

Vocabulary
- synonyms
- sight words

Grammar
- adjectives
- quotation marks

Handwriting
- lowercase cursive letters

Here are some activities you and your child might enjoy.

Amusing Attributes Riddles such as the following are great ways to exercise your child's thinking skills. Read each riddle and ask your child to figure out the common link.

Abby likes books . . . but not reading. She likes swimming . . . but not splashing. Abby likes napping . . . but not dozing. She also enjoys spaghetti . . . but not pasta. (Abby likes things that have double letters.)

Alex likes apples . . . but not fruit. He likes airplanes . . . but not jets. Alex likes August . . . but not summer. He also enjoys astronomy . . . but not stars. (Alex likes things that start with "A".)

What's Your Estimate? Ask your child to estimate how many times in 60 seconds he or she can . . .
a) say his or her full name   **b)** write the days of the week

Then have him or her try each activity and compare the results with the estimate.

Imagine That! Invite your child to close his or her eyes. Ask: *What sounds do you hear*? Can your child name ten?

Amazing Animals If your child could be any kind of animal, which one would he or she choose and why? Using lots of detail, have your child describe or draw ten reasons.

Your child might enjoy reading the following books:

Angel Child, Dragon Child
by Michele Maria Surat

Stringbean's Trip to the Shining Sea
by Vera B. Williams

The True Story of the Three Little Pigs
by Jon Scieszka

_____ **'s Incentive Chart: Week 3**

Name Here

This week, I plan to read_____ minutes each day.

CHART YOUR PROGRESS HERE.

Week 3 I read for...	Day 1	Day 2	Day 3	Day 4	Day 5
	minutes	minutes	minutes	minutes	minutes
Put a sticker to show you completed each day's work.					

Congratulations!

Wow! You did a great job this week!

#1

Place sticker here.

Parent or Caregiver's Signature_____

a–z

a   b   c   d   e   f   g

h   i   j   k   l   m

n   o   p   q   r   s   t

u   v   w   x   y   z

Write.

Describe a Noun

An **adjective** describes a person, place, or thing. Color, size, and number words are adjectives.

Read each sentence. Find the adjective and the noun it describes. Circle the noun. Write the adjective on the line.

1. Peggy and Rosa went to the big zoo. _____

2. They looked up at the tall giraffe. _____

3. The giraffe looked down at the two girls. _____

4. The giraffe had brown spots. _____

Write adjectives from the sentences in the chart.

Color Word	Size Words	Number Word
_____	_____	_____
	_____	

Scholastic Inc.   Summer Express: Between Grades 2 & 3

Panda Pair

In 1972, Americans fell in love with two giant pandas named Hsing-Hsing and Ling-Ling. The pandas came to the United States from China. The National Zoo in Washington, D.C., became the pandas' new home. On their first day there, 20,000 people visited the two pandas. The crowds kept coming year after year.

Hsing-Hsing and Ling-Ling were just cubs when they got to the United States. As the years passed, many hoped the pair would have cubs of their own. Ling-Ling gave birth several times. But none of the babies lived more than a few days. Each time a cub died, people around the world felt sad.

Both pandas lived to an old age. Ling-Ling was 23 when she died in 1992. Hsing-Hsing died in 1999 at the age of 28. But the pandas were not forgotten. At the National Zoo, the glass walls of their home were covered with letters from children. The letters expressed the children's love for the pandas and told how much they were missed.

1. **The author wrote this passage mostly to:**
    A. tell about Hsing-Hsing and Ling-Ling.
    B. explain where giant pandas come from.
    C. describe a giant panda's cubs.
    D. convince people to visit the National Zoo.

2. **According to the author, how did people feel about the pandas?**

_____

3. **If you visited the National Zoo in 2000, what would you have seen at the pandas' home?**

_____

Number Words

Write each sentence using numbers and symbols.

1. Four plus five is nine.	
2. Eleven minus six is five.	
3. Nine plus seven is sixteen.	
4. Four plus eight is twelve.	
5. Three minus two is one.	
6. Seven plus seven is fourteen.	
7. Fifteen minus ten is five.	
8. Two plus eight is ten.	
9. Five minus two is three.	

Scholastic Inc.   Summer Express: Between Grades 2 & 3

Who Is Speaking?

Quotation marks show the exact words someone says. They go before the speaker's first word. They also go after the speaker's last word and the end punctuation mark.

Read each sentence. Underline the exact words the speaker says. Put the words in quotation marks. The first one is done for you.

1. Max said, "Let's go on a picnic."

2. Cori replied, That's a great idea.

3. Andy asked, What should we bring?

4. Max said with a laugh, We should bring food.

5. Cori added, Yes, let's bring lots and lots of food.

6. Andy giggled and said, You're no help at all!

Finish the sentences below by writing what Max, Cori, and Andy might say next. Use quotation marks.

7. Max said, _____.

8. Cori asked, _____.

9. Andy answered, _____.

Same As. . .

Circle the correct word to complete each sentence.

1. A stick is like a stake, and a cap is like a _____.

   A. sock   B. hat   C. twig

2. A runner is like a racer, and a smile is like a _____.

   A. frown   B. face   C. grin

3. A crowd is like a mob, and a song is like a _____.

   A. group   B. tune   C. flute

4. A dinner is like a supper, and a pot is like a _____.

   A. pan   B. cook   C. meal

5. Fur is like fuzz, and wet is like _____.

   A. messy   B. dry   C. damp

6. Sad is like gloomy, and happy is like _____.

   A. glad   B. mad   C. nice

7. Misty is like foggy, and fast is like _____.

   A. runner   B. quick   C. slow

8. Look is like see, and sleep is like _____.

   A. nap   B. wake   C. find

 Discuss with someone in your family why you did not choose the other words.

Scholastic Inc.   *Summer Express: Between Grades 2 & 3*

Sandwich Shop

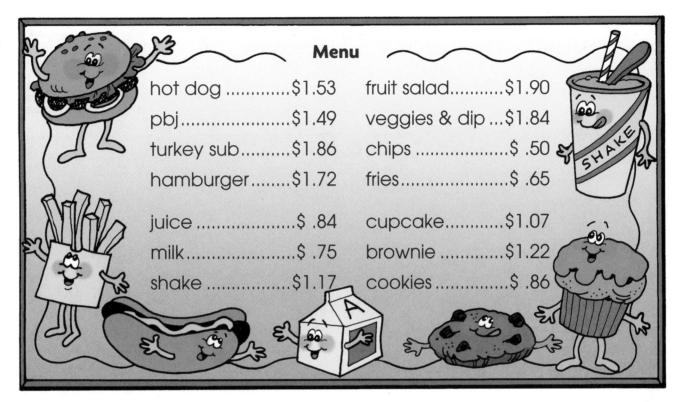

Menu

hot dog $1.53	fruit salad...........$1.90
pbj....................$1.49	veggies & dip ...$1.84
turkey sub.........$1.86	chips ....$ .50
hamburger.......$1.72	fries....................$ .65
juice ....$ .84	cupcake............$1.07
milk....................$ .75	brownie $1.22
shake $1.17	cookies...............$ .86

Add.

A.

pbj
chips
milk
brownie   + _____

B.

hamburger
fries
shake   + _____

C.

turkey sub
veggies & dip
juice
cupcake   + _____

D.

hot dog
fruit salad
brownie
juice   + _____

E.

turkey sub
chips
shake   + _____

F.

pbj
cookies
milk   + _____

Celebrating Our Country

Draw a picture of something you do to celebrate the Fourth of July.

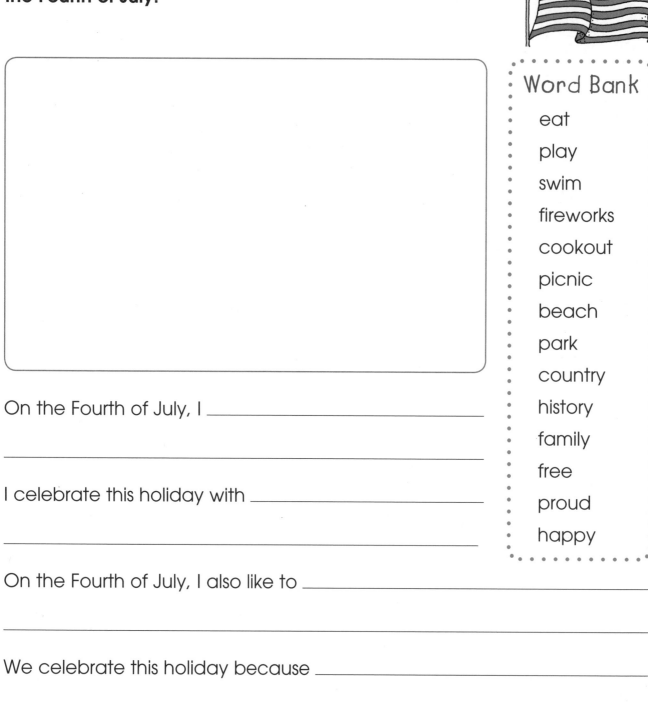

Word Bank

eat
play
swim
fireworks
cookout
picnic
beach
park
country
history
family
free
proud
happy

On the Fourth of July, I _____

_____

I celebrate this holiday with _____

_____

On the Fourth of July, I also like to _____

_____

We celebrate this holiday because _____

_____

Scholastic Inc.   Summer Express: Between Grades 2 & 3

Sort It Out!

Put each word from the Word Box in the circle where it belongs.
We did the first one for you.

Word Box

~~found~~	find	behind
away	upon	pull
call	put	above
below	around	

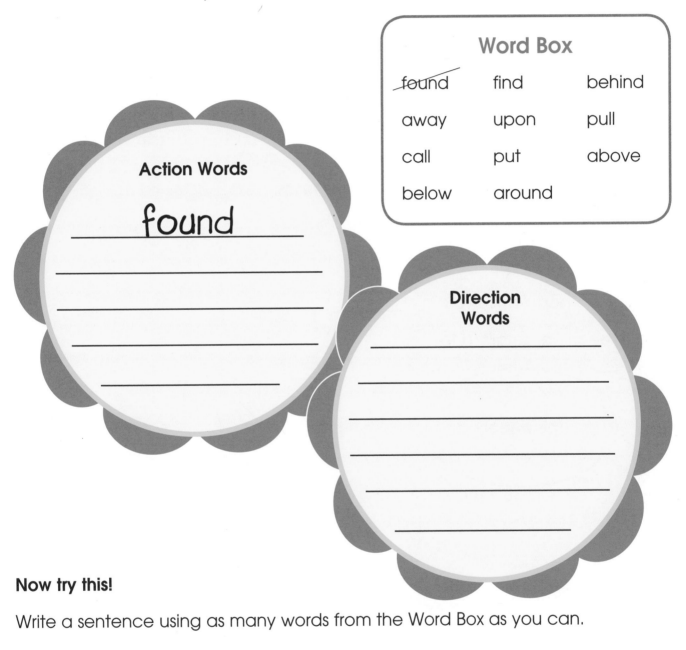

Action Words

found

_____

_____

_____

_____

Direction Words

_____

_____

_____

_____

_____

Now try this!

Write a sentence using as many words from the Word Box as you can.

_____

_____

How many words from the Word Box did you use? _____

Fancy Fireworks

Kaboom! It's the Fourth of July. Fireworks light up the night. Have you ever seen a willow firework? It has long trails of color that float to the ground. The pinwheel and comet are two other popular fireworks. One of the loudest fireworks is called the salute. After a bright flash, you hear a loud BOOM!

Read the paragraph. Then answer the questions.

1. Which firework has long trails of color? _____

2. Which firework makes a loud BOOM? _____

3. What is a popular firework? _____

Add three more details to the web.

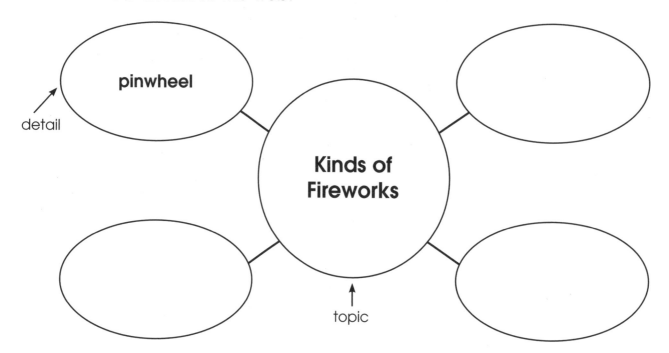

detail

pinwheel

Kinds of Fireworks

topic

 What do you think a pinwheel firework looks like? Draw a picture to show your ideas.

Scholastic Inc.   Summer Express: Between Grades 2 & 3

Helping Your Child Get Ready: Week 4

These are the skills your child will be working on this week.

Math
- measurement
- multiplication

Reading
- reading for details
- comprehension

Writing
- expanding sentences
- adjectives

Vocabulary
- sight words

Grammar
- subject/verb agreement
- past tense

Here are some activities you and your child might enjoy.

Compound Interest Point out examples of compound words to your child. Then have him or her keep track of the compound words heard during an hour. Try it another time and challenge your child to improve on his or her last "score."

Start Collecting Having a collection is a great way for a child to develop higher-level thinking skills like sorting and analyzing. Encourage your child to start one. Leaves, rocks, stamps, or shells are all easy and fun things to collect. Your child can also practice comparing and contrasting by discussing how the items in his or her collection are similar and different from one another.

The Case of the Mysterious Sock Invite your child to find a secret object to put in a sock. Try to guess what it is by feeling the object through the sock. Trade places. Play again.

Pet Autobiography Suggest that your child write the story of your pet's (or an imaginary pet's) life. The story should be an autobiography—from the pet's point of view!

Your child might enjoy reading the following books:

Dinner at Aunt Connie's House
by Faith Ringgold

The Family Under the Bridge
by Natalie Savage Carlson

Ramona Quimby, Age 8
by Beverly Cleary

_____ 's Incentive Chart: Week 4

Name Here

This week, I plan to read_____ minutes each day.

CHART YOUR PROGRESS HERE.

Week 4 I read for...	Day 1 minutes	Day 2 minutes	Day 3 minutes	Day 4 minutes	Day 5 minutes
Put a sticker to show you completed each day's work.					

Congratulations!

Wow! You did a great job this week!

Place sticker here.

Parent or Caregiver's Signature_____

What's for Lunch?

Have you ever had a string bean sandwich? Most students wouldn't want that for lunch! What is the favorite sandwich in America's school lunches? If you said peanut butter and jelly, you'd be right. Other popular sandwiches are ham and bologna. Cheese is the fourth favorite sandwich. Many students also like turkey sandwiches.

What is the topic of the paragraph?
Write it in the center circle.
Find five details that tell about the topic.
Write them in the web.

 What kinds of sandwiches does your family like the best? Take a survey of your family.

Find the Word

Complete the sentences below with words from the Word Box. Then find the words in the puzzle. Words may go across, down, or diagonally. We did the first one for you.

1. Have you __thought__ about what you'd like for your birthday?

2. Hannah likes to _____ home from school.

3. Last Friday, I _____ a new notebook.

4. Today I will _____ the notebook to school with me.

5. Ruthie and Carlos like to _____ pictures of animals.

6. May I _____ your hand if I get scared during the movie?

7. Sometimes we _____ too loudly in the library.

8. Tanya used colored pencils when she _____ that picture.

B	T	B	R	I	N	G	T
D	H	E	W	E	Q	H	S
R	O	J	O	Z	G	X	K
A	U	O	Q	U	R	L	B
W	G	H	O	E	A	D	P
D	H	B	O	W	M	R	F
P	T	V	K	L	L	E	M
T	A	L	K	S	D	W	F

Word Box

bought	drew
bring	draw
~~thought~~	walk
hold	talk

What Happened?

If the naming part of a sentence is a noun or pronoun that names one, the verb ends in **-s**, except for the pronouns **I** and **you**. If the naming part is a noun or pronoun that names more than one, the verb does not end in **-s**.

Choose the correct action word from the box to complete each sentence. Write it on the line. You may use each word once.

play	run	dive	climb	throw
plays	runs	dives	climbs	throws

1. Mia _____ ball with her friends.

2. The children like to _____ together.

3. Juan _____ faster than I do.

4. We _____ on a track team.

5. Tom and Kara _____ into the pool.

6. Mary _____ without her goggles.

7. They _____ very tall trees.

8. Liz _____ steep mountains.

9. Juan _____ our ball to Mia.

10. I _____ the ball to Juan.

She hops.

They hop.

Football Frenzy

A sentence is more interesting when it gives exact information.

Replace each word to make the sentence more exact.

1. **The** ball **game starts** soon **.**

   The ___soccer___ game starts ___now___.

2. **We are meeting** her there **.**

   We are meeting _____ _____.

3. **Let's eat** this **and** that **before the game.**

   Let's eat _____ and _____ before

   the game.

4. **I hope** they **score** some **points.**

   I hope _____ score _____ points.

5. They **were also** there **.**

   _____ were also _____.

6. He **played a** good **game!**

   _____ played a _____ game!

Scholastic Inc. *Summer Express: Between Grades 2 & 3*

Weight Watcher

Weight can be measured in ounces (oz.) and pounds (lb.). 16 oz. = 1 lb. Which unit of measure would you use to weigh the items below? Underline the more sensible measure.

1. An apple

    ounces   **pounds**

2. A skateboard

    ounces   **pounds**

3. A bar of soap

    ounces   **pounds**

4. A bicycle

    ounces   **pounds**

5. A watermelon

    ounces   **pounds**

6. A baseball player

    ounces   **pounds**

7. A balloon

    ounces   **pounds**

8. A jam sandwich

    ounces   **pounds**

9. A baseball bat

    ounces   **pounds**

10. A pair of socks

    ounces   **pounds**

11. A slice of pizza

    ounces   **pounds**

12. A full backpack

    ounces   **pounds**

13. A large dog

    ounces   **pounds**

14. A loaf of bread

    ounces   **pounds**

15. A paintbrush

    ounces   **pounds**

Lost and Found

Read the story. Then fill in the bubble next to the best answer to each question below.

One day Alisha's little brother found **three** dollars. "Look!" he said. "Now I can buy a pony!"

"I think a pony will cost too **much**," Alisha said. "**Shall** I help you **find** something to spend it on?"

"Okay," he said. He **put** the money in his pocket.

"Ice cream might be a good thing to spend it on," said Alisha. "What **kind** do you want?"

"I **only** like one kind. Chocolate," said her brother.

"I think chocolate is the best kind, **too**," said Alisha.

1. When Alisha says a pony will cost too **much**, she means
   - ○ a. Three dollars is more than enough money to buy a pony.
   - ○ b. A pony costs a lot more than three dollars.
   - ○ c. If her brother had found three dollars, he could buy a pony.

2. When Alisha says, "I think chocolate is the best kind, **too**," the word **too** means
   - ○ a. also.
   - ○ b. two.
   - ○ c. not at all.

3. The opposite of **found** is
   - ○ a. kept.
   - ○ b. forgot.
   - ○ c. lost.

4. Which word means the same as **kind** in this story?
   - ○ a. nice
   - ○ b. child
   - ○ c. type

5. In the dictionary, the word **only** appears
   - ○ a. between the words **lonely** and **quiet**.
   - ○ b. after the word **totally**.
   - ○ c. before the word **night**.

Scholastic Inc.   *Summer Express: Between Grades 2 & 3*

Letter From Vera

April 11

Dear Morey,

   I just got your letter with the picture of you riding your bike. From the smile on your face, I can tell how much fun you're having. I still remember when you could hardly ride a tricycle. You've come a long way!

   Now here's some advice. I'm sure you're a good rider. But you will fall off that bike now and then. So please get yourself a helmet. Wear it every time you ride. A helmet will help protect you from a head injury. Wearing a helmet when you ride a bike is as important as wearing your seat belt when you ride in a car!

   No, I'm not trying to be a bossy know-it-all. I just don't want a bad fall to wipe that smile off your face. When you come to visit this summer, bring your bike and your helmet. We'll take some great rides together!

Your cousin,
Vera

1. **From this letter, what can you tell about the picture of Morey that he sent to Vera?**

   A. He is riding a tricycle.

   B. He is not wearing a helmet.

   C. He is in his driveway.

   D. He is looking scared.

2. **Vera's advice shows that she:**

   F. cares a lot about safety.

   G. is often bossy and mean.

   H. doesn't like riding bikes.

   J. is learning to drive a car.

3. **What will Morey do with Vera during the summer?**

   _____

   _____

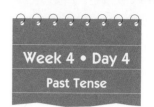
A Verb Puzzle

Verbs tell when action takes place. Past-tense verbs tell about action that happened in the past. Most past-tense verbs end in **-ed**.

Write the past tense of each word in the box. Then use the past tense words to complete the puzzle below.

call _____	mix _____	play _____
yell _____	kick_____	help_____
bark _____	climb _____	walk _____

Across

1. Mike _____ over the wall.
3. The dog _____.
5. Our teacher _____ us with the math problems.
7. We _____ at the team to win.
8. The boys _____ home from school.

Down

1. Sam _____ his dad on the phone.
2. Grandma _____ the cake batter.
4. The player _____ the ball.
6. Marie _____ a game with Zack.

Write a sentence using each of the verbs from the puzzle.

Scholastic Inc. *Summer Express: Between Grades 2 & 3*

How Many Legs?

Fill in the blanks.

1.	How many legs on	

1 turkey _____   3 turkeys _____

2 turkeys _____   4 turkeys _____

2.	How many legs on	

1 cat _____   3 cats _____

2 cats _____   4 cats _____

3.	How many legs on	

1 ladybug _____   3 ladybugs _____

2 ladybugs _____   4 ladybugs _____

4.	How many legs on	

1 spider _____   3 spiders _____

2 spiders _____   4 spiders _____

5.	How many legs on	

1 squid _____   6 squid _____

2 squid _____   7 squid _____

3 squid _____   8 squid _____

4 squid _____   9 squid _____

5 squid _____   10 squid _____

Mystery Bags

Adjectives *are words that help you imagine how something looks, feels, smells, sounds, or tastes.*

Make a list of words that describe the object in each bag below.

 Use a paper sack to make a real mystery bag. Place an object in the bag and give describing clues to someone. Can he or she guess the mystery object?

Helping Your Child Get Ready: Week 5

These are the skills your child will be working on this week.

Math
- multiplication
- number words

Reading
- compare/contrast

Writing
- combining sentences

Vocabulary
- homophones
- proofreading/spelling

Grammar
- verbs
- contractions

Handwriting
- cursive numbers 0–9

The New Bike
By Cindy Read
illustrations by Ana Rest

Here are some activities you and your child might enjoy.

Carrot-Turnip-Pea Develop your child's listening skills by creating a word chain. In this game, someone says a word, and the next person must say a word that begins with the last letter of the previous player's word. To make this more challenging, try choosing a category such as names or foods.

Now You See It, Now You Don't Show your child an interesting picture and ask him or her to look at it for a minute. Then turn the picture over and ask your child to list the objects that he or she can remember on a sheet of paper. If you wish, allow your child to look at the picture for another minute and then add more items to the list. For a twist, use a picture with less detail, but ask your child to list the words in alphabetical order.

Secret Messages Suggest that your child come up with a code to write secret messages. Have him or her trade messages with you or another family member.

Can You Judge a Book by Its Cover? Give your child a chance to create a new cover for a favorite book. Remind him or her to include the title, as well as the names of the author and any illustrator. Encourage your child to include an image or images that he or she thinks would inspire someone to read the book.

Your child might enjoy reading the following books:

The Summer My Father Was Ten
by Pat Brisson

This Land Is Your Land
by Woody Guthrie

Falling Up
by Shel Silverstein

_____ **'s Incentive Chart: Week 5**

Name Here

This week, I plan to read_____ minutes each day.

CHART YOUR PROGRESS HERE.

Week 5	Day 1	Day 2	Day 3	Day 4	Day 5
I read for...	minutes	minutes	minutes	minutes	minutes
Put a sticker to show you completed each day's work.					

  Congratulations!

Wow! You did a great job this week!

Place sticker here.

Parent or Caregiver's Signature _____

Foreign Flags

Every country has its own flag. Japan has a white flag with a red circle on it. The red circle stands for the sun. Japan's name means the "land of the rising sun." Canada also has a red and white flag. But its flag has a white background with two wide red stripes. In the center of the flag is a red maple leaf. The maple tree is a symbol of Canada.

Read the paragraph. Then answer the questions.

1. What colors are both flags? _____

2. What does Japan's flag have in the center? _____

3. What does Canada's flag have in the center? _____

4. How are the backgrounds of the two flags different? _____

_____

Write your answers in the correct parts of the circles.

 Find Japan and Canada on a world map.

Verb *to be*

Am, **is**, **are**, **was**, and **were** are forms of the verb **to be**. These verbs show being instead of action.

Read each sentence. Underline the verb. Write **past** if the sentence tells about the past. Write **now** if the sentence tells about the present.

1. The story is perfect.   _____

2. The producers are happy.   _____

3. The actors were funny.   _____

4. The movie studio is interested in the story.   _____

5. I am excited about the movie.   _____

6. I was sad at the end.   _____

Scholastic Inc. *Summer Express: Between Grades 2 & 3*

Numbers 0-9

Trace and write.

0   0

1   1

2   2

3   3

4   4

5   5

6   6

7   7

8   8

9   9

Field Trip Cars

1. Josie's class is going to the teddy bear factory.
   Three children will ride in each car.
   Draw a circle around the children who will ride in each car.

   How many cars do they need? _____

2. Pete's class is going to see the elephant seals.
   Five children will ride in each van.
   Draw a circle around the children who will ride in each van.

   How many vans do they need? _____

3. Rosa's class is going to the Space Museum.
   Eight children will ride in each small bus.
   Draw a circle around the children who will ride in each bus.

   How many small buses do they need? _____

Scholastic Inc.   Summer Express: Between Grades 2 & 3

Contractions With *not*

A **contraction** is two words made into one word. An **apostrophe** takes the place of the missing letter or letters. In a contraction, **not** becomes **n't**.

Read each sentence. Write a contraction for the underlined words.

1. Cindy and Ed <u>could not</u> bake a cake.   _____

2. There <u>was not</u> enough flour.   _____

3. They <u>are not</u> happy.   _____

4. <u>Do not</u> give up!   _____

5. They <u>did not</u> give up.
   They made cupcakes!   _____

Write a sentence using a contraction you wrote.

_____

_____

Chilly or Chili?

 Homophones *are words that sound the same but are spelled differently and have different meanings.*

Write the correct homophone in each blank to complete the sentences.

1. **bored, board**
   Some of the _____ members seemed

   quite _____ at the last meeting.

2. **bare, bear**
   When a _____ cub is born, it is _____,
   and its eyes are closed.

3. **chilly, chili**
   Nothing tastes better than a bowl of _____ on a _____ day.

4. **guest, guessed**
   Who would have _____ that your _____ was a thief!

5. **patients, patience**
   I wonder if doctors ever lose their _____ with difficult _____.

On another sheet of paper, rewrite each sentence using the correct homophones.

6. I'll meat you at ate inn the mourning.

7. Would ewe fix me sum tee and a bowl of serial?

8. My ant and uncle lived oversees four too years in Madrid.

9. Alex was sick with the flue and mist a hole weak of school.

10. I want two bye a knew pear of shoes, but I dew knot have a sent left.

Scholastic Inc. *Summer Express: Between Grades 2 & 3*

A State Apart

The state of Michigan has two parts—the Upper Peninsula and the Lower Peninsula. Peninsulas are long arms of land that jut into water. Both of Michigan's peninsulas are almost surrounded by the Great Lakes. The Upper Peninsula has many big forests. It is also rich in minerals. The Lower Peninsula has more people and large cities. Most of the state's industry is in the Lower Peninsula. Both peninsulas attract tourists who come to spend vacations in Michigan.

Read the paragraph. Add headings to the Venn diagram. Then write facts in each part of the diagram.

 The Lower Peninsula of Michigan is larger in area than the Upper Peninsula. Add this fact to the diagram.

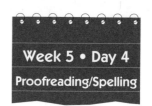
Garage Sale

Find and mark the ten spelling errors.

We have grate stuff and big bargains!

Office Supplys

- Big boxes of old newspaper
- Ballpoint pens that are out of ink
- Broken rubber bands
- Empty printer ink containers

Clothing

- Singel left shoes
- Socks with hoales
- Jackets with broken zippers
- Sleeves that were cut off a shirt

Household Goods

- Old phon books
- Torn sheets
- Old toothbrushes
- Empty pante cans
- Chipped plates
- A bunch of old pizza boxs

Ferniture and Hardware

- A big box of bent nails
- A saggy bed
- A sofa with mice living in it
- A chare with only three legs
- A TV with only one channel
- Old dor knobs

Scholastic Inc.   Summer Express: Between Grades 2 & 3

Cow Code

Riddle: Where do cows go for entertainment?

What to Do

Find the corresponding numerals below. Then use the Decoder to solve the riddle by filling in the spaces at the bottom of the page. The first one has been done for you.

1. nine   **9**

2. twenty-two

3. seventeen

4. forty-five

5. sixty-seven

6. one hundred eight

7. eighty-six

8. one hundred fifty-three

9. three hundred seventy

10. five hundred thirty-four

Decoder

23	X
17	O
153	E
21	A
370	O
108	S
76	D
9	V
15	F
67	T
22	E
435	P
86	H
88	R
45	I
534	M
118	W
543	N
307	G

TO __ __ __ " __ __ __ " v __ __ __ __
    5   7   2   10   3   9   1   4   8   6

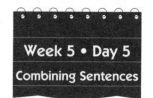
Cake and Ice Cream

 Two sentences that share the same subject can be combined to make one sentence by using the word and.

Rewrite the sentences by combining their endings.

1. The party was fun.
   The party was exciting.

   The party was fun and exciting.

2. We blew up orange balloons.
   We blew up red balloons.

3. We ate cake.
   We ate ice cream.

4. The cake frosting was green.
   The cake frosting was yellow.

5. We made a bookmark.
   We made a clay pot.

6. We brought games.
   We brought prizes.

Scholastic Inc.   *Summer Express: Between Grades 2 & 3*

Helping Your Child Get Ready: Week 6

These are the skills your child will be working on this week.

Math
- place value
- telling time

Reading
- comprehension
- compare/contrast

Writing
- building sentences

Vocabulary
- rhyming words

Grammar
- verbs
- pronouns
- adjectives

Here are some activities you and your child might enjoy.

Mapping My World Invite your child to draw pictures and write labels to make maps of familiar places, such as his or her school, a local park, or a favorite friend's home.

Word Expert Boost your child's vocabulary by playing Word Expert. Tell him or her that for each word you say, he or she must give you an antonym and a synonym, as well as an example of the word. For instance, if you say *exciting*, a synonym might be *thrilling*, an antonym might be *boring*, and an example could be *riding a rollercoaster*.

Nutrition Label Math Show examples of food labels to your child, ideally those with more than one serving in a package. Talk about what the numbers on the label mean. Then ask your child to determine the nutrition totals for the entire item. For example, if there are 2 servings in a small can of vegetables, your child can double the nutrition label numbers to find the total calories, fat and carbohydrate content, and so on.

One-Minute Categories Ask your child to name as many examples as possible of a category in one minute. For example, for animals, he or she might name dog, cat, wolf, tiger, and so on. Make the categories more challenging as his or her skill increases. You can also specify naming animals that starts with a particular letter. For example, for the letter *d*, animals would include dog, duck, and donkey.

Your child might enjoy reading the following books:

Amber Brown Is Not a Crayon
by Paula Danziger

How to Be Cool in the Third Grade
by Betsy Duffey

Mice and Beans
by Pam Muñoz Ryan

_____ **'s Incentive Chart: Week 6**
Name Here

This week, I plan to read_____ minutes each day.

CHART YOUR PROGRESS HERE.

Week 6 I read for...	Day 1	Day 2	Day 3	Day 4	Day 5
	minutes	minutes	minutes	minutes	minutes
Put a sticker to show you completed each day's work.					

Congratulations!

Wow! You did a great job this week!

#1

Place sticker here.

Parent or Caregiver's Signature_____

Cleaning the Alligator's Teeth

The alligator asked if I
Would clean his dirty teeth.
I climbed inside his jagged jaws
And brushed up underneath.

I felt his two jaws start to close.
His sharp teeth touched my skin.
I yelled, "I'm not a sandwich!
Open up and give a grin!"

The alligator laughed and made
His two jaws open wide.
I said, "The next time you do that
I'll have to pinch your hide."

He gave another 'gator laugh
That shook me head to toe.
I finished brushing all his teeth
And said, "I've got to go."

★ SPECIAL WORDS ★

clean	jaws	start	grin	wide	stood

Cleaning the Alligator's Teeth

Reading Comprehension

Fill in the blanks with the word that best completes the sentence.

1. The alligator asked if I would clean his dirty _____ .

   claws   teeth   scales   tail

2. I climbed inside his jagged _____ .

   nose   ears   mouth   jaws

3. I felt his two jaws start to _____ .

   open   chew   lick   close

4. His _____ teeth touched my skin.

   many   white   sharp   mean

5. I yelled, "I'm not a sandwich! Open up and give a
   _____ !"

   laugh   grin   yell   bite

Rhyme Time

Circle the words in each column that rhyme with the word in bold. What other words rhyme with that word? Write them on the lines below.

clean	jaws	start	grin	wide	stood
bean	claws	dart	win	wind	good
mean	jam	star	fin	hide	stop
seen	laws	cart	pin	ride	hood
_____	_____	_____	_____	_____	_____
_____	_____	_____	_____	_____	_____

Colorful Fish

Look at the numbers in the shapes inside the fish.

Use the information in the key at right to color the shapes.

If there is a . . .	Color the space . . .
6 in the tens place	green
5 in the hundreds place	blue
2 in the ones place	yellow
7 in the tens place	orange
9 in the hundreds place	red

Verbs *have*, *had*

The verb **to have** is irregular. Use **have** or **has** to tell about the present. Use **had** to tell about the past.

Choose the correct word from the chart to complete each sentence.

In the Present	In the Past
have, has	had

1. Joe _____ new running shoes.

2. I _____ new shoes, too.

3. Last week we _____ old shoes.

4. I _____ a green shirt on.

5. Joe _____ a blue shirt on.

6. Yesterday we both _____ red shirts on.

7. Last year we _____ to walk to the park.

8. Now, I _____ skates.

9. Now, Joe _____ a bike.

Scholastic Inc.   Summer Express: Between Grades 2 & 3

Get Your Ticket!

Write a sentence to match each picture. Be sure to include a subject, an action, and a part that tells where or when.

1. A boy climbs a tree in his backyard.

2. _____

3. _____

 Find a cartoon in the newspaper. Use the pictures to write a sentence on another sheet of paper. Be sure to include a subject, an action, and a part that tells where or when.

Slide Show

 A sentence is more interesting when it includes a subject, an action, and a part that tells where or when.

Write three sentences and draw pictures to match.

subject	action	where or when

1. _____

subject	action	where or when

2. _____

subject	action	where or when

3. _____

 Switch the sentence parts around to make three silly sentences! Write the sentences on another sheet of paper.

Scholastic Inc.   *Summer Express: Between Grades 2 & 3*

Play Ball

What's your favorite ball game? Many people like sports in which they throw a ball. In bowling and basketball, you throw a ball. Other people play games in which they hit a ball. Golf and tennis are two examples. Still another game in which a ball is hit is lacrosse. A third kind of ball game calls for kicking a ball. Players kick balls in soccer, football, rugby, and of course, kickball.

Read the paragraph. Then answer the questions.

1. What are four sports where you kick a ball? _____

2. What are three sports in which you hit a ball? _____

3. In what games do you throw a ball? _____

Use your answers to complete the chart.

Hitting a Ball	Throwing a Ball	Kicking a Ball

 What do you do with the ball in baseball? Add baseball to the chart.

Send In the Subs

A **pronoun** is a word that can take the place of a noun.

The nouns in these sentences need a rest. Pick a pronoun to replace the underlined word(s). Then write the sentence with the pronoun.

Pronoun Subs					
he	you	we	they	it	she

1. <u>Tanya</u> swings the bat.

   _____

2. <u>Mr. Bartlet and Mr. Jones</u> blow their whistles.

   _____

3. <u>Matt and I</u> warm up.

   _____

4. <u>Leo</u> looks for his glove.

   _____

5. <u>The ball</u> rolls into the field.

   _____

Check your sentences. Did you begin them with a capital letter?

Scholastic Inc.   Summer Express: Between Grades 2 & 3

Prime Timer

Write the time 3 ways.

example: 1:15
15 minutes after 1
45 minutes to 2

1. _____

_____ minutes after _____

_____ minutes to _____

2. _____

_____ minutes after _____

_____ minutes to _____

4. <image clock>

3. _____

_____ minutes after _____

_____ minutes to _____

4. _____

_____ minutes after_____

_____ minutes to _____

6. <image clock>

5. _____

_____ minutes after _____

_____ minutes to _____

6. _____

_____ minutes after _____

_____ minutes to _____

Describing a Surprise

Use adjectives to describe an object.

Read the words on the box.
What do they describe?

_____

| white | high |
| puffy | moving |

Think of a surprise to hide in each box. Then write four adjectives to describe it.

1.

2.

3.

4.

Read your adjectives to a friend. Can your friend guess what the surprise is?
If not, can you think of better adjectives?

80

Helping Your Child Get Ready: Week 7

These are the skills your child will be working on this week.

Math
- fractions
- using arrays

Reading
- comprehension
- compare/contrast
- cause and effect

Writing
- combining sentences
- verb usage

Vocabulary
- sight words/verbs
- prefixes/*un-*

Grammar
- sentence punctuation
- comparative/superlative

Here are some activities you and your child might enjoy.

Compliment Jar Create a compliment jar by labeling a clear plastic jar with the word "Compliments". Invite everyone in your home to write a compliment for another family member on a slip of paper and place it in the jar. Once a week, invite your child to read the compliments aloud to the rest of the family. For a twist, turn it into a guessing game. Your child can read the compliment but leave out the name. Can anyone guess this person's identity? Your child can provide clues, if necessary.

List-en Up Help your child develop good listening and memorization skills. Read a list of five items two times. Then ask your child to repeat the list back to you in order. Here is a list of the Great Lakes (in alphabetical order) to get you started: Lake Erie, Lake Huron, Lake Michigan, Lake Ontario, Lake Superior.

Character Friends Ask your child to talk about a character in one of the books he or she has been reading. You can prompt the discussion by asking questions like these: *Which characters would you want to be friends with in real life? What are some of the good qualities this character has? How are you and the character similar or different?*

Summer Games Plan a mini "Summer Olympics" with your family. Play classic picnic games such as a water-balloon toss or a three-legged race, or make up fun games of your own. Take turns trying them!

Your child might enjoy reading the following books:

American Tall Tales
by Mary Pope Osborne

In the Year of the Boar and Jackie Robinson
by Betty Bao Lord

Tiger Math: Learning to Graph From a Baby Tiger
by Ann Whitehead Nagda

_____ 's Incentive Chart: Week 7

Name Here

This week, I plan to read _____ minutes each day.

CHART YOUR PROGRESS HERE.

Week 7	Day 1	Day 2	Day 3	Day 4	Day 5
I read for...	minutes	minutes	minutes	minutes	minutes
Put a sticker to show you completed each day's work.					

Congratulations!

Wow! You did a great job this week!

Place sticker here.

Parent or Caregiver's Signature _____

Fraction Fun

Something that is split in 2 equal parts is divided in "half."

These two shapes are divided in half.

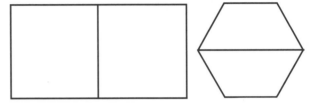

> **A fraction has a number on the top:** ⟶ **1**
>
> **A fraction has a number on the bottom, too:** ⟶ **2**
>
> **The top number tells the "fraction," or parts, of the whole.**
>
> **The bottom number tells the number of parts in the whole.**

A. **Draw a line to match the picture with a fraction.**

$\dfrac{2}{2}$ $\dfrac{2}{12}$ $\dfrac{2}{3}$

B. **The top number in these fractions tells you how many parts to color. Try it!**

color $\dfrac{1}{2}$ color $\dfrac{2}{2}$

Statements and Questions

A **statement** is a sentence that tells something. It ends with a period.
A **question** is a sentence that asks something. It ends with a question mark.

A. Read each sentence. Write Q on the line if the sentence is a question.
Write S if the sentence is a statement.

1. Where did the ant live? _____

2. The ant had many cousins. _____

3. She found the crumb under a leaf. _____

4. How will she carry it? _____

5. Who came along first? _____

6. The lizard wouldn't help. _____

7. He said he was too cold. _____

8. Why did the rooster fly away? _____

B. The sentences below do not make sense. Rewrite the words in the
correct order.

1. How crumb did carry the ant the?

_____

_____

2. She herself it carried.

_____

_____

Scholastic Inc.   *Summer Express: Between Grades 2 & 3*

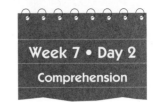

Blending In

How are the following words alike: *blue, black, blink*? If you said they all begin with *bl*, you're right. Some other words that begin with these letters are *blob, blanket,* and *blimp*. Letter pairs like *bl* are "blends." Blends are two or more consonants that work together. What blend do the following words begin with: *green, gray, grumpy*? Two other blends are *tr* and *sm*. Words such as *smoke, smile, try, tray, smack, trick, truck,* and *smell* begin with these blends.

Use the paragraph to write four headings for the chart. Then write examples under each heading.

 Add at least two more words to each group on the chart.

Great Gardening Tips

Sentences can also be combined to make them more interesting. Key words can help put two sentences together.

old: I will plan my garden. I am waiting for spring.

new: I will plan my garden while I am waiting for spring.

Write a new sentence using the key word in each flower.

1. Fill a cup with water. Add some flower seeds.

   _____

2. This will soften the seeds. They are hard.

   _____

3. Fill a cup with dirt. The seeds soak in water.

   _____

4. Bury the seeds in the cup. The dirt covers them.

   _____

5. Add water to the plant. Do not add too much.

   _____

6. Set the cup in the sun. The plant will grow.

   _____

Scholastic Inc.   Summer Express: Between Grades 2 & 3

A-maze-ing Verbs

To complete the maze, pass only through the correct sentences. An incorrect sentence is like a wall in the maze: You cannot pass through it. The correct path takes you through nine boxes.

Three Nests

You can use **adjectives** to compare things. To compare two things, add -er to the adjective. To compare three or more things, add -est.

Biddie Bird has a friend named Betty. Betty always wants to outdo Biddie. If Biddie has a clean nest, Betty has a cleaner nest. Biddie and Betty have another friend named Birdie. She likes to outdo both Biddie and Betty. So she has the cleanest nest.

Read the sentences. Then fill in the chart so the correct form of each adjective is under each bird's name.

Biddie	Betty	Birdie
clean	cleaner	cleanest
1. _____	_____	_____
2. _____	_____	_____
3. _____	_____	_____
4. _____	_____	_____
5. _____	_____	_____
6. _____	_____	_____

1. Betty's nest is <u>newer</u> than Biddie's.

2. Biddie has a <u>small</u> nest.

3. Birdie has the <u>warmest</u> nest of all.

4. Biddie's nest is <u>round</u>.

5. Birdie built the <u>neatest</u> nest.

6. Betty has a <u>softer</u> nest than Biddie.

On another sheet of paper, use the words you wrote on the chart to draw a picture of each bird's nest.

Scholastic Inc.   Summer Express: Between Grades 2 & 3

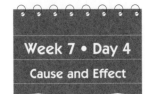

Fool the Birds

A woman in Virginia had a problem. Birds ate all the seeds she carefully planted. The woman put brown belts along the newly planted rows in her garden. Just as she had hoped, the birds thought the belts were snakes! As a result, the birds stayed out of the garden. The woman's plants grew in peace.

Read the paragraph. Then complete the cause-and-effect map.

Other Effects

Cause

First Effect

 MORE! What conclusions can you make about birds and snakes?

Banana-Rama

Color the word that is missing from each sentence
and write it on the line.

1. We _____ a spelling test yesterday.   taked   took

2. There _____ frost on the ground.   was   were

3. Tommy _____ the Statue of Liberty.   seen   saw

4. How _____ elephants are at the zoo?   much   many

5. Carla _____ her lizard to school.   brought   brang

6. Have you _____ my dog?   seen   saw

7. Alyssa _____ a new pair of skates.   gots   has

8. You _____ supposed to finish your work.   are   is

9. We _____ standing near a snake!   were   was

10. They _____ a pig in the mud.   seen   saw

11. We _____ our winter boots.   wore   weared

12. Is she _____ to come over?   gonna   going

13. _____ your cat climb trees?   Do   Does

14. Rosie _____ cookies to the bake sale.   brang   brought

Scholastic Inc.   Summer Express: Between Grades 2 & 3

A Ray of Fun

An **array** demonstrates a multiplication sentence. The first **factor** tells how many rows there are. The second **factor** tells how many there are in each row. The answer of a multiplication sentence is called the **product**.

2 x 4 = 8   ○ ○ ○ ○   2 rows
              ○ ○ ○ ○   4 in each row

Write the multiplication sentence for each array.

A.   ○ ○ ○
     ○ ○ ○

B.   ○ ○ ○
     ○ ○ ○
     ○ ○ ○

C.   ○ ○
     ○ ○
     ○ ○
     ○ ○

D.   ○ ○ ○ ○ ○
     ○ ○ ○ ○ ○
     ○ ○ ○ ○ ○

_____   _____   _____   _____

E.   ○ ○ ○

F.   ○ ○ ○
     ○ ○ ○
     ○ ○ ○
     ○ ○ ○

G.   ○ ○ ○ ○ ○ ○
     ○ ○ ○ ○ ○ ○

H.   ○ ○ ○ ○
     ○ ○ ○ ○
     ○ ○ ○ ○

_____   _____   _____   _____

I.   ○ ○ ○ ○ ○ ○
     ○ ○ ○ ○ ○ ○
     ○ ○ ○ ○ ○ ○

J.   ○ ○ ○
     ○ ○ ○
     ○ ○ ○
     ○ ○ ○
     ○ ○ ○

K.   ○
     ○
     ○
     ○

L.   ○ ○
     ○ ○
     ○ ○
     ○ ○
     ○ ○
     ○ ○

_____   _____   _____   _____

 It was time for our family photo. The photographer arranged us into four rows. There were six people in each row. How many people in all were in the photo? On another sheet of paper, draw an array to solve this problem.

How Unusual!

The prefix **un-** means either "not" or "do the opposite of" the base word. Circle each base word in the puzzle. The words go →, ↓, ↗, and ↘. We did the first one for you.

| un~~pack~~ | untie | unload | unlock | unwind | undo |
| unknown | unfold | unable | unfair | unusual | unwise |

R	A	I	L	I	M	A	F	X
N	E	E	O	F	F	O	L	D
I	W	E	A	W	A	X	L	E
A	I	X	D	L	I	I	O	T
T	S	K	N	O	W	N	R	N
R	E	V	O	C	Z	R	D	I
E	(P	A	C	K)	X	E	A	A
C	A	B	L	E	S	Y	Z	P
D	N	I	K	U	S	U	A	L

Write a word from the list to complete each sentence.

1. It is _____ for James to be late for school.

2. It took me ten minutes to _____ the knot.

3. You need a key to _____ the trunk.

4. We grew more concerned as the story began to _____.

5. It is _____ to wait until the last minute to do your homework.

6. Bill thought the umpire's call was _____.

Helping Your Child Get Ready: Week 8

These are the skills your child will be working on this week.

Math
- fractions
- multiplication

Reading
- finding the main idea
- reading for details
- comprehension

Vocabulary
- proofreading/spelling
- sight words

Writing
- sequencing
- commas

Grammar
- singular and plural nouns
- sentence types

Here are some activities you and your child might enjoy.

Spinning Stories Cut out ten pictures from a magazine. Put them in a bag. Invite your child to take them out two or three at a time and use the pictures to tell a story.

20 Questions This favorite game can be used to build thinking skills. First choose a category, such as animals. Then think of one animal. Tell your child that he or she can ask only "yes" or "no" questions to determine the animal you are thinking of. Once he or she gets the hang of it, take turns thinking of an animal while the other asks questions.

Going Acrostic Provide opportunities for your child to create "acrostic" poems. To begin an acrostic poem, first write any word vertically (you may wish to start with your child's name). Then your child uses each letter of the word as the first letter in another word—one that relates to the original word—and writes that word horizontally.

Food Fractions Fractions are fun to practice using foods like pizza or various fruits. With your child, define the whole item. Then divide it in half, quarters, eighths, or more. What is the smallest piece you can make?

Your child might enjoy reading the following books:

Charlotte's Web
by E.B. White

The Mouse and the Motorcycle
by Beverly Cleary

The Wright Brothers at Kitty Hawk
by Donald J. Sobol

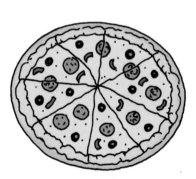

_____**'s Incentive Chart: Week 8**

Name Here

This week, I plan to read _____ minutes each day.

CHART YOUR PROGRESS HERE.

Week 8 I read for...	Day 1	Day 2	Day 3	Day 4	Day 5
	minutes	minutes	minutes	minutes	minutes
Put a sticker to show you completed each day's work.	◯ ◯	◯ ◯	◯ ◯	◯ ◯	◯ ◯

Congratulations!

Wow! You did a great job this week!

#1

Place sticker here.

Parent or Caregiver's Signature _____

How to "Ride" a Poem

Find and mark the ten spelling errors.

Writeing a poem

Is like riding a bike

Once you start riding,

You ride where you like.

For exampel, I can write

Any wurd I want here,

As long as it rhymes

And soundes good to the ear.

I can write in any style

I can write in any spede,

As long as my readrs

Continue to read.

There'is only one danger,

One risk that I run,

When I sense that my readers

Have stoped having fun.

At this point its' best

Not to delay

Simply kick up your kickstand

And just ride eway.

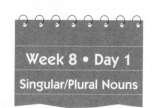

One, or More

A **singular noun** names one person, place, or thing. A **plural noun** names more than one person, place, or thing. Add **-s** to form the plural of most nouns.

A. Each sentence has an underlined noun. On the line, write S if it is a singular noun. Write P if it is a plural noun.

1. She has a new <u>baby</u>.   _____

2. <u>It</u> is very cute.   _____

3. She has small <u>fingers</u>.   _____

4. She drinks from a <u>bottle</u>.   _____

5. I can tell my <u>friends</u> all about it.   _____

B. Read each sentence. Underline the singular noun. Circle the plural noun.

1. The baby has two sisters.

2. The nightgown has pockets.

3. Her hand has tiny fingers.

4. My parents have a baby.

5. The father has three girls.

C. Complete the chart. Write the singular or plural of each noun.

Singular	Plural
fence	
	trains
gate	
	cows

96

Scholastic Inc.   *Summer Express: Between Grades 2 & 3*

The Milky Way

 The **main idea** of a story tells what the story is mostly about. **Details** in a story tell more information about the main idea.

What do you think of when you hear the words, "Milky Way?" Do you think of a candy bar? Well, there is another Milky Way, and you live in it! It is our galaxy. A galaxy is a grouping of stars. Scientists have learned that there are many galaxies in outer space. The Milky Way is a spiral-shaped galaxy with swirls of stars spinning out from the center of it. Scientists believe there are about 200 billion stars in the Milky Way. In our solar system, many planets orbit the sun. One of them is Earth. Even from Earth, on a clear night away from city lights, you can see part of the Milky Way. It is called that because so many stars close together look like a milky white stripe across the sky. However, if you looked at it with a telescope, you would see that it is made up of thousands of stars.

Complete the main idea and each detail about the story.

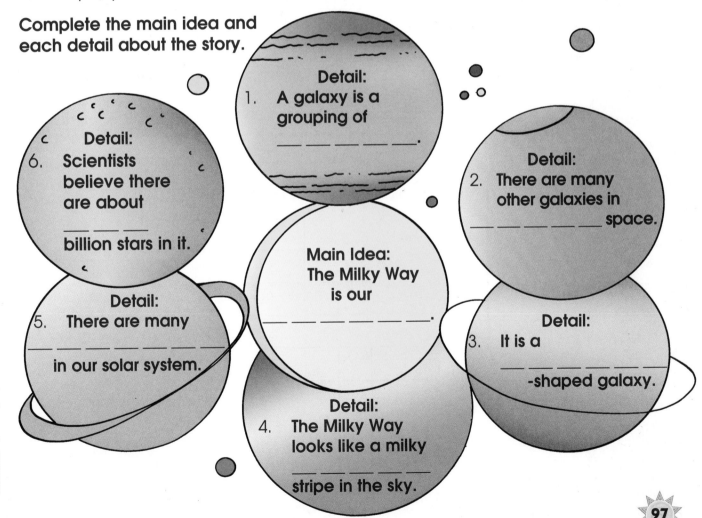

Detail:
1. A galaxy is a grouping of
_ _ _ _ _ _ _ .

Detail:
6. Scientists believe there are about
_ _ _ _
billion stars in it.

Detail:
2. There are many other galaxies in
_ _ _ _ _ _ space.

Main Idea:
The Milky Way is our
_ _ _ _ _ _ _ .

Detail:
5. There are many
_ _ _ _ _ _
in our solar system.

Detail:
3. It is a
_ _ _ _ _ _
-shaped galaxy.

Detail:
4. The Milky Way looks like a milky
_ _ _ _ _ _
stripe in the sky.

Puzzle It Out!

Use the words in the Word Box to complete the sentences below.
Then write the words in the correct spaces in the puzzle.

Across

1. My name was the first

   _____ that I learned to spell.

3. Sam washed the dishes so they were

   sparkling _____.

4. The weather today is _____

   but not hot.

5. At the end of second grade, our

   teacher said we were _____

   for third.

Down

2. Will you share my popcorn, or do

   you want your _____?

3. She has to _____ the baby

   because he's too little to walk.

6. We had burgers for dinner last

   night, and we're having them

   _____ tonight.

Word Box

carry	warm
own	clean
again	word
ready	

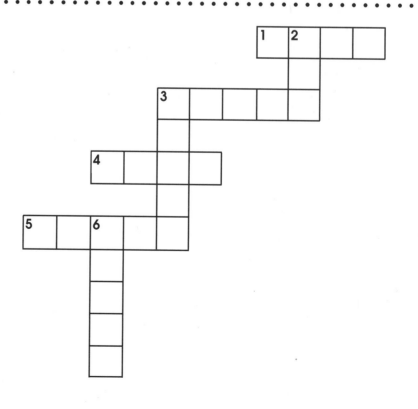

Scholastic Inc.   *Summer Express: Between Grades 2 & 3*

More Fun With Fractions

A fraction has two numbers. The top number tells the parts of the whole.
The bottom number tells how many total parts there are.

A. $\frac{10}{10}$ is the whole circle.

Color $\frac{8}{10}$ of the circle.

How much is not colored? ____

B. $\frac{10}{10}$ is the whole rectangle.

Color $\frac{4}{10}$ of the rectangle.

How much is not colored? ____

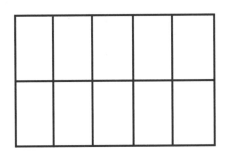

$$\frac{10}{10} - \frac{8}{10} = \underline{}$$

$$\frac{10}{10} - \frac{4}{10} = \underline{}$$

C. Solve this fraction equation. Cross out the dogs to help you.

$$\frac{10}{10} - \frac{3}{10} = \underline{}$$

Exclamations and Commands

An **exclamation** is a sentence that shows strong feeling.
A **command** is a sentence that gives an order.

A. Read each sentence. Write E on the line if the sentence is an exclamation.
   Write C if the sentence is a command.

1. They chase buffaloes! _____

2. You have to go, too. _____

3. Wait at the airport. _____

4. It snows all the time! _____

5. Alligators live in the sewers! _____

6. Look at the horse. _____

7. That's a great-looking horse! _____

8. Write a letter to Seymour. _____

B. Complete each exclamation and command.

1. I feel _____!

2. Help your _____.

3. That's a _____!

4. I lost _____!

5. Turn the _____.

6. Come watch the _____.

7. Please let me _____.

Scholastic Inc.   *Summer Express: Between Grades 2 & 3*

Lulu to the Rescue

VOLUME X   Anyplace, USA   **Monday, June 11**

JoAnne Altsman always thought her pet pig LuLu was a good companion. Now she also thinks of LuLu as a hero. Why? When JoAnne suffered a heart attack in 1998, LuLu saved her life.

JoAnne was vacationing in her camper when she fell ill. She yelled for help, but no one heard her cries. LuLu knew that JoAnne was in trouble. She pushed through a dog door and ran to the road. She tried to stop passing cars but had no luck. LuLu hurried back to the camper three times to see how JoAnne was.

At last LuLu did something drivers were sure to notice. She lay down on the road and stuck her feet in the air. Finally, a car stopped. The driver got out and followed LuLu back to the camper. JoAnne heard the man knocking on the door. "There's something wrong with your pig!" he yelled.

"There's something wrong with me!" JoAnne yelled back. "Call 911!"

Before long, help was on its way. Today JoAnne is well, and she's grateful for her pet pig. Without LuLu, she would have died.

1. Where was JoAnne when she fell ill?
   A. on vacation
   B. at school
   C. in her home
   D. at work

2. Why did LuLu push her way out of the camper and run to the road?

   _____

3. "LuLu was a good companion." What is a companion?
   F. guard
   G. nurse
   H. doctor
   J. friend

4. What probably happened after the man knocked on the door of the camper? Tell two things that probably happened.

   _____

   _____

Stories of Nature

 Sentences should be written in the correct order to tell a story.

Finish the stories by writing a sentence about each of the last two pictures.

First: Two birds build a nest.

Next: _____

Last: _____

First: A flower bud grows.

Next: _____

Last: _____

Scholastic Inc.   *Summer Express: Between Grades 2 & 3*

Time to Group

 The multiplication symbol (x) can be thought of as meaning "groups of."

3 "groups of" 4 equals 12
3 x 4 = 12

5 "groups of" 2 equals 10.
5 x 2 = 10

Write the multiplication sentence for each diagram.

A.

_____

B.

_____

C.

_____

D.

_____

E.

_____

F.

_____

G.

_____

H.

_____

I.

_____

J.

_____

K.

_____

L.

_____

M.

_____

N.

_____

O.

_____

P.

_____

 William has five bags of hamburgers. There are seven hamburgers in each bag. On another sheet of paper, draw pictures to show the total number of hamburgers.

The Sky's the Limit

➡️ *Some sentences include a list. A* **comma** *(,) is used to separate each item in the list.*

For example: Mrs. Jones asked the class to work on pages two, three, and four.

Fill in the blanks to make a list in each sentence. Watch for commas!

1. I ate _____, _____,
   and _____ for breakfast.

2. We stayed with Grandma on _____,
   _____, and _____ nights.

3. I found _____, _____,
   and _____ in my party bag.

4. The boys played _____,
   _____, and _____
   at summer camp.

5. The _____, _____,
   and _____ ate the corn we scattered.

6. The pigs built their houses using _____,
   _____, and _____.

💡 **Cut a balloon shape out of paper. On one side, list three objects that fly. On the other side, write a sentence that lists the objects shown on the right side of this page.**

Scholastic Inc.   *Summer Express: Between Grades 2 & 3*

Helping Your Child Get Ready: Week 9

These are the skills your child will be working on this week.

Math
- multiplication
- bar graph

Reading
- sequencing
- following directions

Writing
- proofreading
- sentence fragments

Vocabulary
- word relationships
- common phrases

Grammar
- common and proper nouns
- adjectives

Here are some activities you and your child might enjoy.

Math in a Menu When you and your child are looking at a menu, take the opportunity to practice math concepts. Ask questions like these: *Which food item costs the most? How much is it? Which item costs the least? If you bought the most expensive and the least expensive items, how much would you spend altogether?*

Summer Fun With A–Z Ask your child to think about what he or she loves about summer. Then challenge him or her to write about these things in sentences that use all 26 letters of the alphabet. Encourage your child to circle each letter the first time it is used.

Double Meanings Reinforce the concept of homophones with your child by challenging him or her to find two (or more!) meanings for each of these words: bob, fair, lock, pitcher. Come up with more homophones to challenge your child further.

How Puzzling! Invite your child to create a jigsaw puzzle. Provide a large sheet of paper, crayons or colored markers, and scissors. First your child can draw a picture. Then he or she can cut it up into smaller pieces and mix them up. See if you, or another family member can put it back together!

Your child might enjoy reading the following books:

Charlie and the Chocolate Factory
by Roald Dahl

So You Want to Be President?
by Judith St. George

Tea With Milk
by Allen Say

_____ **'s Incentive Chart: Week 9**
Name Here

This week, I plan to read _____ minutes each day.

CHART YOUR PROGRESS HERE.

Week 9 I read for...	Day 1	Day 2	Day 3	Day 4	Day 5
	minutes	minutes	minutes	minutes	minutes
Put a sticker to show you completed each day's work.	◯ ◯	◯ ◯	◯ ◯	◯ ◯	◯ ◯

Congratulations!

Wow! You did a great job this week!

Place sticker here.

Parent or Caregiver's Signature _____

The Father of Our Country

After you finish reading, go back and look for mistakes.

Use the proofreading marks to correct eight mistakes in the letter.

<u>m</u>ars = **Make a capital letter.**   ? = **Add a question mark.**   ! = **Add an exclamation point.**

. = **Add a period.**   ⸲ = **Add a comma.**

Dear Friend,

my job as the first president of the United States was hard My friends and I had to make new laws new money, and new jobs. the capital was in New York when I became president. then it moved to Philadelphia. Is the capital still there. Who is the president today! I would love to see how the United States has changed over the past two hundred years?

Sincerely,

George Washington

On another sheet of paper, write a letter to today's president.
The White House address is: 1600 Pennsylvania Avenue, Washington, D.C. 20500.

Adding Quickly

 The addition sentence 4 + 4 + 4 + 4 + 4 = 20 can be written as a multiplication sentence. Count how many times 4 is being added together. The answer is 5. So, 4 + 4 + 4 + 4 + 4 = 20 can be written as 5 x 4 = 20. Multiplication is a quick way to add.

Write a multiplication sentence for each addition sentence.

A. 5 + 5 + 5 = 15

B. 6 + 6 + 6 + 6 = 24

C. 8 + 8 = 16

D. 2 + 2 + 2 + 2 = 8

E. 7 + 7 + 7 = 21

F. 4 + 4 + 4 + 4 = 16

G. 9 + 9 + 9 = 27

H. 5 + 5 + 5 + 5 + 5 = 25

I. 3 + 3 + 3 + 3 + 3 = 15

J. 10 + 10 + 10 + 10 = 40

K. 1 + 1 + 1 + 1 + 1 = 5

L. 11 + 11 + 11 = 33

M. 8 + 8 + 8 + 8 = 32

N. 0 + 0 + 0 + 0 = 0

O. 12 + 12 + 12 + 12 = 48

P. 9 + 9 + 9 + 9 = 36

 Today, we are going to the beach. Mom packed the picnic basket with six sandwiches, six water bottles, six candy bars, and six apples. How many items did she pack in all?

Scholastic Inc. *Summer Express: Between Grades 2 & 3*

Common or Proper?

A **common noun** names any person, place, or thing. A **proper noun** names a particular person, place, or thing. A proper noun begins with a capital letter.

A. Is the underlined word a common noun or a proper noun?
Write *common* or *proper*.

1. The <u>girl</u> likes to learn. _____

2. She goes to two <u>schools</u>. _____

3. She lives in <u>America</u>. _____

B. Underline the common nouns. Circle the proper nouns.

1. April has a brother and a sister.

2. Their names are Julius and May.

3. Their parents were born in Taiwan.

4. April goes to school on Saturday.

5. She is learning a language called Mandarin.

6. May read a book about the Middle Ages.

C. Underline the common nouns. Circle the proper nouns.
Then write them on the chart in the correct category.

1. Last August David went to camp.

2. Many children go to a picnic on the Fourth of July.

Common Nouns	**Proper Nouns**
_____	_____
_____	_____
_____	_____

Dinnertime

 A **sentence** is a group of words that expresses a complete thought.
A **fragment** is an incomplete thought.

Write *S* for sentence or *F* for fragment.

_____ 1. Insects eat many different things.

_____ 2. Some of these things.

_____ 3. The praying mantis eats other insects.

_____ 4. Waterbugs eat tadpoles and small frogs.

_____ 5. Flower nectar makes good.

_____ 6. Nests to store their food.

_____ 7. The cockroach will eat almost anything.

_____ 8. Termites.

_____ 9. A butterfly caterpillar.

_____ 10. Animals and people.

_____ 11. Some insects will even eat paper.

_____ 12. Insects have different mouth parts to help them eat.

On another sheet of paper, write about three things you did during the day using only sentence fragments. Have someone read it. Did they understand it? Why or why not?

Scholastic Inc.   Summer Express: Between Grades 2 & 3

Scrambled Eggs

 Sequencing *means putting the events of a story in the order in which they happened.*

The sentences below are scrambled. Number them in the correct sequence.

A. ____ I took a shower.
   ____ I got out of bed.
   ____ I got dressed.

B. ____ She planted the seeds.
   ____ Big pink flowers bloomed.
   ____ Tiny green shoots came up.

C. ____ He ate the sandwich.
   ____ He spread some jelly on them.
   ____ He got out two pieces of bread.

D. ____ He slid down the slide.
   ____ He climbed up the ladder.
   ____ He landed on his feet.

E. ____ We built a snowman.
   ____ Low gray clouds drifted in.
   ____ It began to snow hard.

F. ____ Firefighters put out the fire.
   ____ Lightning struck the barn.
   ____ The barn caught on fire.

G. ____ The pepper spilled out of
         the jar.
   ____ I sneezed.
   ____ My nose began to itch.

H. ____ "My name is Emma."
   ____ "Hi, what is your name?"
   ____ "It's nice to meet you, Emma."

I. ____ I said, "Okay, do a trick first."
   ____ Rover whined for a treat.
   ____ I gave him a dog biscuit.
   ____ He danced on his hind legs.

J. ____ She built a nest.
   ____ Baby birds hatched from
         the eggs.
   ____ I saw a robin gathering straw.
   ____ She laid four blue eggs.

Adjectives

An **adjective** is a word that describes a person, place, or thing.

A. Read each sentence. Write the adjective that describes the underlined noun on the line.

1. We live near a sparkling <u>brook</u>. _____

2. It has clear <u>water</u>. _____

3. Large <u>fish</u> swim in the brook. _____

4. Busy <u>squirrels</u> play near the brook. _____

5. You can enjoy breathing in the fresh <u>air</u> near the brook. _____

B. Complete each sentence by adding an adjective.

1. I love _____ apples.

2. I see a _____ ball.

3. I smell _____ flowers.

4. I hear _____ music.

5. I like the _____ taste of pickles.

 Write three sentences that tell about the foods you like the best. Use adjectives in your description.

Scholastic Inc. *Summer Express: Between Grades 2 & 3*

Sneaky Snakes

Snakes are very good at hiding. Most snakes can **camouflage** themselves into their environment. That means they have different colors and patterns on their bodies that allow them to blend in with the colors and patterns of things around them. Camouflage helps them hide from their enemies and helps them be **sneaky** when they are trying to capture something to eat. For example, the emerald tree boa lives in the **jungle**. Its green skin makes it nearly invisible among the green leaves of the trees. **Rattlesnakes** live in rocky, dry places. The patterns of black, tan, and brown on their backs help them blend in with their rocky environment. The horned viper lives in the desert. Its skin is the same color as **sand** where it burrows underground. It is hard to see unless it is moving. Also, some snakes that are harmless look very similar to **venomous** snakes. The harmless milk snake is colored orange, with yellow and black stripes, much like the poisonous **coral snake**. The enemies of the milk snake mistake it for a coral snake because they look so much alike.

Find the answers in the story. Write them in the puzzle.

1. Write the word that starts with a *v* and means "poisonous."

2. Write another word for "tricky."

3. Write what helps a snake blend in with its surroundings.

4. Write where emerald tree boas live.

5. Write what snakes live in rocky places and have black, tan, and brown patterned skin.

6. Write what is the same color as the horned viper.

7. Write the name of the snake that looks like a milk snake.

Write the letters from the numbered squares in the puzzle above to fill in each box.

How It Is

Circle the word that best completes each sentence and write it on the line.

1. An ant is black, and a grasshopper is _____.
   A. blue   B. fuzzy   C. green

2. A shirt is cotton, and a jar is _____.
   A. glass   B. silk   C. jam

3. A hill is rolling, and a river is _____.
   A. winding   B. rainy   C. steep

4. A daisy is white, and a rose is _____.
   A. green   B. dirty   C. red

5. A ring is round, and a box is _____.
   A. wool   B. square   C. happy

6. An elephant is large, and a mouse is _____.
   A. small   B. huge   C. yellow

7. A puddle is muddy, and a pool is _____.
   A. sad   B. clear   C. shy

8. A hammer is hard, and a pillow is _____.
   A. sleepy   B. sharp   C. soft

Discuss with someone why you did not choose the other words.

Scholastic Inc.   Summer Express: Between Grades 2 & 3

"Fun and Games"

 Some words like "hammer and nails" and "salt and pepper" just go together.

Choose a word from the box to

sooner	right
chips	sweet
order	lost
sugar	effect
bacon	fun
shine	business
error	easy
name	gentlemen
cup	alive
cents	pots

1. cause and _____

2. _____ and games

3. _____ and saucer

4. cream and _____

5. _____ and found

6. _____ and address

7. ladies and _____

8. law and _____

9. _____ and sour

10. nice and _____

11. trial and _____

12. _____ and pans

13. fish and _____

14. rain or _____

15. _____ or pleasure

16. _____ or wrong

17. dead or _____

18. dollars and _____

19. _____ and eggs

20. _____ or later

 On another sheet of paper, list three other pairs of words that go together.

Great Graphing

A. How many pennies equal 5¢? How many nickels equal 5¢?
   Color in the boxes on the graph to show your answers.

Pennies										
Nickels										
	1	2	3	4	5	6	7	8	9	10

B. How many pennies equal 10¢? How many nickels equal 10¢? How many
   dimes equal 10¢? Color in the boxes on the graph to show your answers.

Pennies										
Nickels										
Dimes										
	1	2	3	4	5	6	7	8	9	10

C. How many pennies equal 25¢? How many nickels equal 25¢?
   How many quarters equal 25¢? Color in the boxes on the graph to
   show your answers.

Pennies
Nickels
Quarters
1 2 3 4 5 6 7 8 9 10 11 12 13 14 15 16 17 18 19 20 21 22 23 24 25

Scholastic Inc.   *Summer Express: Between Grades 2 & 3*

Helping Your Child Get Ready: Week 10

These are the skills your child will be working on this week.

Math
- division
- geometric shapes

Reading
- cause and effect

Writing
- punctuating questions

Vocabulary
- antonyms
- compound words

Grammar
- adjectives
- possessives
- prepositions

Here are some activities you and your child might enjoy.

Snappy Summaries Writing a summary is often hard for children. To help your child sharpen this important skill, have him or her create one-sentence summaries of favorite books, movies, or television shows. To do this, have your child answer this question: *Who did what, when, and why?* This may take a bit of practice!

Comic Mix-Up Build up your child's sequencing skills. Cut a comic strip into sections. Ask your child to put the strip in the correct order and to explain his or her thinking.

Wonderful Window Invite your child to look out of a window. Then ask: *What do you see that begins with the letter W?* See if your child can name five things. You can try this with other letters as well.

Travel Brochure Together, you and your child can create a "travel brochure" for someplace you have been over the summer. For example, the place could be something as local as a neighborhood swimming pool or park, or a distant place that was part of a big vacation. Write about the place (or places) and remember to include pictures, either illustrated, images found in magazines, or if possible, real photographs.

Your child might enjoy reading the following books:

Rent a Third Grader
by B. B. Hiller

The Scrambled States of America
by Laurie Keller

Ten True Animal Rescues
by Jeanne Betancourt

Special Note: The activity for Day 4 of this week is a mini-book. Have your child tear out the page along the perforation and cut along the dotted line. After he or she positions the two sections so the mini-book pages are in sequence, have your child staple and fold to form a book. Then he or she can complete all the puzzles in the mini-book.

_____**'s Incentive Chart: Week 10**

Name Here

This week, I plan to read_____ minutes each day.

CHART YOUR PROGRESS HERE.

Week 10	Day 1	Day 2	Day 3	Day 4	Day 5
I read for...	minutes	minutes	minutes	minutes	minutes
Put a sticker to show you completed each day's work.					

Congratulations!

Wow! You did a great job this week!

#1

Place sticker here.

Parent or Caregiver's Signature_____

Buckets of Fun

 An **adjective** *helps you imagine how something looks, feels, smells, sounds, or tastes.*

Write a list of adjectives on each bucket to fit the bucket's category.

words that describe size

_____

_____

_____

words that describe taste or smell

_____

_____

_____

words that describe sounds

_____

_____

_____

words that describe how something feels

_____

_____

_____

words that describe weather

_____

_____

_____

words that describe feelings

_____

_____

_____

 Make a "mystery bag" by putting a secret object inside. Tell someone about the object inside using describing words!

Candy Boxes

Steve works in a candy store. He puts candy into boxes. Each box has 10 spaces. Steve has 32 candies. Try to draw 32 candies in the boxes below. Write the number of candies in each box on the line. Write the number of any leftover candy at the bottom of the page.

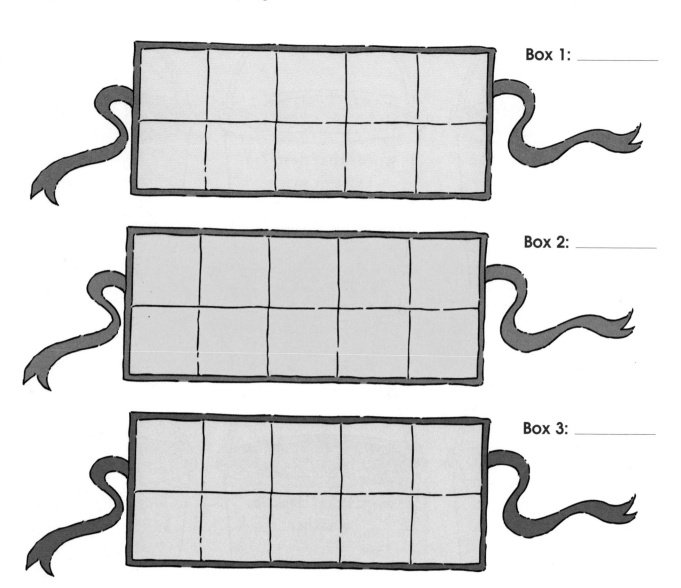

Box 1: _____

Box 2: _____

Box 3: _____

Scholastic Inc.   Summer Express: Between Grades 2 & 3

Whose Is It?

A **noun** can show who owns something. To do this, add an **(')** and **-s**.

Joe is packing for a trip. He needs to pack everything on the list. Each object belongs to a different family member. Study the picture to learn who owns each thing. Then write it on the suitcase.

skateboard   hat   bone
bowl   sunglasses   teddy bear

1. _____   4. _____

2. _____   5. _____

3. _____   6. _____

On another sheet of paper, write a story about Joe's family and their trip.

The Opposite Of. . .

Circle the correct word to complete each sentence and write it on the line.

1. Rich is the opposite of poor, and weak is the opposite of _____.

    A. strong   B. day   C. frail

2. Give is the opposite of take, and ask is the opposite of _____.

    A. get   B. answer   C. teacher

3. Help is the opposite of harm, and work is the opposite of _____.

    A. hurt   B. try   C. play

4. Good is the opposite of bad, and rough is the opposite of _____.

    A. smooth   B. bumpy   C. mean

5. Over is the opposite of under, and near is the opposite of _____.

    A. middle   B. far   C. here

6. Warm is the opposite of cool, and safe is the opposite of _____.

    A. afraid   B. cold   C. unsafe

7. Cloudy is the opposite of sunny, and early is the opposite of _____.

    A. late   B. day   C. timely

8. Top is the opposite of bottom, and front is the opposite of _____.

    A. whole   B. back   C. side

 Discuss with someone why you did not choose the other words.

Scholastic Inc.   Summer Express: Between Grades 2 & 3

Where Is It?

A **preposition** often helps tell where something is.

Study the picture. Find each item in the column on the left. Then draw a line to the words that tell where it is. The prepositions are underlined.

What	**Where**
1. chair	a. <u>above</u> the door
2. bear	b. <u>on</u> the desk
3. shoe	c. <u>under</u> the bed
4. plane	d. <u>behind</u> the trash basket
5. cat	e. <u>in</u> the bed
6. computer	f. <u>at</u> the window
7. dog	g. <u>near</u> the desk
8. poster	h. <u>over</u> the bed

Pick three objects from the picture and write a complete sentence to tell where each object is.

Wacky World

An asking sentence is called a **question**. It begins with a capital letter and ends with a question mark (**?**).

Write each question correctly.

1. **why is that car in a tree**

_____

2. **should that monkey be driving a bus**

_____

3. **did you see feathers on that crocodile**

_____

4. **can elephants really lay eggs**

_____

5. **is that my mother covered in spots**

_____

 On another sheet of paper, draw your own picture of a wacky world. Write two questions about your picture.

Scholastic Inc.   Summer Express: Between Grades 2 & 3

pen	play	hog	chair	high	window
stick	ground	wheel	arm	deep	way
yard	back	melon	lid	pit	drive
fall	water	brow	eye	ever	green
up	hot	ball	round	lash	house

Compound Roundup

Make as many compound words as you can by joining words in boxes that connect vertically, horizontally, or diagonally. Write your answers on a separate sheet of paper. **There are 20 compound words to round up in each puzzle.**

Name _____

fit	cycle	line	hall	flag	trip
motor	out	air	bell	way	pole
law	cap	side	knob	door	cone
burn	sun	walk	shoe	bone	pine
set	hot	shine	wish	fire	back

weed	shell	shore	stage	dragon	hole
food	sea	sick	fly	coach	scotch
top	cave	fire	proof	hop	butter
sand	car	man	place	fruit	vine
mail	box	shade	lamp	apple	grape

2

mill	wind	toe	tail	light	work
lady	bug	pig	pony	print	step
spread	bed	chop	class	mate	foot
tub	robe	room	stick	stool	mare
cold	bath	mush	way	time	night

4

pick	paste	ache	line	fore	over
drop	tooth	bird	head	how	moon
gum	cage	brush	some	light	saw
day	red	hair	thing	any	guard
home	dream	cut	body	life	where

5

cuffs	shake	wear	every	stand	drop
fog	hand	ship	under	rain	card
kick	horn	pants	bow	board	fold
drum	ache	time	black	cup	bill
ear	stick	lip	cake	spoon	tea

7

skate	pull	quake	worm	pea	pit
board	over	blue	earth	suit	cock
surf	score	due	man	snow	case
bag	end	bench	see	storm	brief
week	bean	work	home	thing	brain

Where the Sun Shines

Florida is known for its pleasant weather. In fact, it has earned the nickname "Sunshine State." As a result of its warm, sunny climate, Florida is a good place for growing fruits, such as oranges and grapefruits. Many older people go to live in Florida. They enjoy the good weather. Northerners on vacation also visit Florida for the same reason.

Read the paragraph. Then complete the cause-and-effect map.

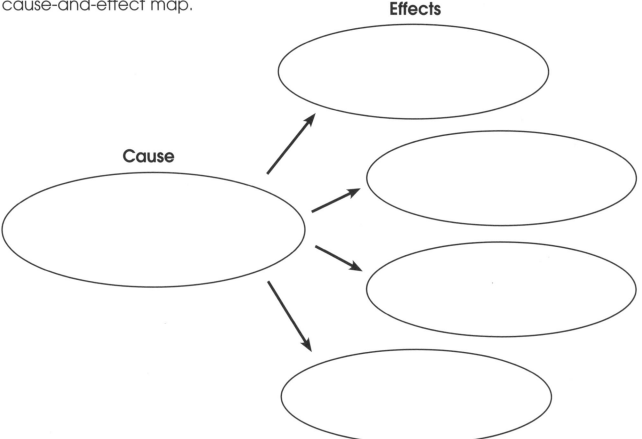

Effects

Cause

MORE! During which season do most people probably go to Florida? Tell why you think so.

Shape Sleuth

Read the riddle. Then circle the answer.

1. I have no corners. I look more like a baseball than a dime.

   a. square

   b. circle

   c. sphere

2. I have three corners and three sides. I look like a sail on a small boat.

   a. pentagon

   b. cylinder

   c. triangle

3. I have six sides. I look more like a gift box than a newspaper.

   a. pyramid

   b. hexagon

   c. rectangular prism

4. Put me on my side and I can roll. I look like a soup can.

   a. cylinder

   b. cube

   c. circle

5. I look like a party hat and something that stops traffic.

   a. square

   b. cone

   c. sphere

6. I have four sides. I look more like a door than a building.

   a. triangle

   b. octagon

   c. rectangle

Scholastic Inc.   *Summer Express: Between Grades 2 & 3*

Answer Key

Week 1

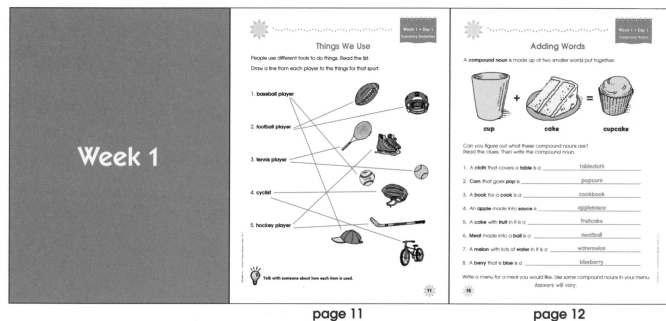

page 11

Things We Use

People use different tools to do things. Read the list.
Draw a line from each player to the things for that sport.

1. baseball player
2. football player
3. tennis player
4. cyclist
5. hockey player

Talk with someone about how each item is used.

page 12

Adding Words

A **compound noun** is made up of two smaller words put together.

cup + cake = cupcake

Can you figure out what these compound nouns are?
Read the clues. Then write the compound noun.

1. A **cloth** that covers a **table** is a _____ tablecloth
2. **Corn** that goes **pop** is _____ popcorn
3. A **book** for a **cook** is a _____ cookbook
4. An **apple** made into **sauce** is _____ applesauce
5. A **cake** with **fruit** in it is a _____ fruitcake
6. **Meat** made into a **ball** is a _____ meatball
7. A **melon** with lots of **water** in it is a _____ watermelon
8. A **berry** that is **blue** is a _____ blueberry

Write a menu for a meal you would like. Use some compound nouns in your menu.
Answers will vary.

---

page 13

Kaleidoscope

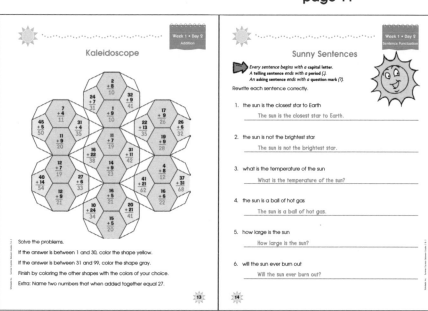

Solve the problems.
If the answer is between 1 and 30, color the shape yellow.
If the answer is between 31 and 99, color the shape gray.
Finish by coloring the other shapes with the colors of your choice.
Extra: Name two numbers that when added together equal 27.

page 14

Sunny Sentences

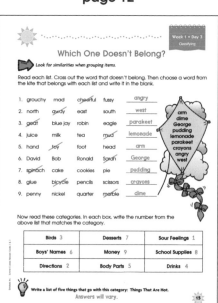

Every sentence begins with a capital letter.
A telling sentence ends with a period (.).
An asking sentence ends with a question mark (?).
Rewrite each sentence correctly.

1. the sun is the closest star to Earth
   The sun is the closest star to Earth.

2. the sun is not the brightest star
   The sun is not the brightest star.

3. what is the temperature of the sun
   What is the temperature of the sun?

4. the sun is a ball of hot gas
   The sun is a ball of hot gas.

5. how large is the sun
   How large is the sun?

6. will the sun ever burn out
   Will the sun ever burn out?

page 15

Which One Doesn't Belong?

Look for similarities when grouping items.

Read each list. Cross out the word that doesn't belong. Then choose a word from
the kite that belongs with each list and write it in the blank.

1. grouchy   mad   cheerful   fussy   — angry
2. north   away   east   south   — west
3. goat   blue jay   robin   eagle   — parakeet
4. juice   milk   tea   mud   — lemonade
5. hand   toy   foot   head   — arm
6. David   Bob   Ronald   Sarah   — George
7. spinach   cake   cookies   pie   — pudding
8. glue   bicycle   pencils   scissors   — crayons
9. penny   nickel   quarter   marble   — dime

arm
dime
George
pudding
lemonade
parakeet
crayons
angry
west

Now read these categories. In each box, write the number from the
above list that matches the category.

Birds	3	Desserts	7	Sour Feelings	1
Boys' Names	6	Money	9	School Supplies	8
Directions	2	Body Parts	5	Drinks	4

Write a list of five things that go with this category: Things That Are Hot.
Answers will vary.

---

page 16

A Happy Camper

Complete:
Every sentence begins with a _____ capital letter .
A statement ends with a _____ period .
A question ends with a _____ question mark .

Uh oh! Dalton was in a hurry when he wrote this letter. Help him find 10 mistakes.
Circle them.

Dear Mom and Dad,
Camp is so cool today we went swimming do
you know what the best part of camp is I think
fishing is my favorite thing to do. did you feed my
hamster I really miss you

Love, Dalton

Now choose two questions and two statements from Dalton's letter. Rewrite
each correctly.

1. _____
2. _____
3. _____
4. _____

Sentences will vary.

On another sheet of paper, write a letter to a friend or family member.
Include two statements and two questions.

page 17

Super Star

Solve the problems. If the answer is between 1 and 20, color the shape yellow.
If the answer is between 21 and 40, color the shape white. If the answer is
between 41 and 90, color the shape blue.

Write five subtraction problems that have answers between 10 and 20.

page 18

Hello, Island!

About 30 years ago, some fishermen
were on their boat near Iceland.
Suddenly they saw smoke coming
from the sea. Then the top of a
volcano rose out of the water. Soon
red-hot rock began to pour down
its sides. It looked like the sea was
on fire. At last the volcano cooled
down. It became a new island.
People named the island Surtsey.

Read how the island of Surtsey was made. Show the correct order of what
happened. Write the numbers from 1–4 on the lines.

2 Red-hot rock poured down its sides.
1 Smoke came out of the sea.
4 The new island was named Surtsey.
3 The volcano cooled down.

Fill in the circles in order. Use the numbers and sentences above to help
you. The first one is done for you.
Check your child's work.

1. Smoke came out of the sea.
2.
3.
4.

Tell someone how Surtsey became an island.
Draw pictures to show what happened.

page 19

Turn on the Lights

Lighthouses warn ships that are near land. The first lighthouses were fires. People would build the fires on hilltops along the coast. Later people built towers. The light from their candles could be seen from far away. Then oil lamps were used. Today electricity runs a lighthouse's powerful lamps.

lamp
tower

Read how lighthouses changed.

Show the correct order of what happened. Write the numbers from 1–4 on the lines.

3 Oil lamps lit lighthouses.
4 Lighthouses use electric light.
1 Fires were built on hillsides.
2 Candles were used.

Fill in the circles in order. Use the numbers and sentences above to help you.

Check your child's work.

1 → 2 → 3 → 4

MORE! Read *The Little Red Lighthouse* and the *Great Gray Bridge* by Hildegarde Swift.

19

---

page 20

Find the Word

Complete the sentences below with words from the Word Box. Then find the words in the puzzle. Words may go across, down, or diagonally. We did the first one for you.

1. I chose a pumpkin that had no bumps and was perfectly **round**
2. Sarah had a question about her homework, so she picked up the phone to **call** Tanisha.
3. After Juan ate the hot fudge sundae, his stomach felt very **full**
4. When my mom went **away** on a trip, she sent me postcards.
5. Miko's cat likes to sit **upon** her lap while Miko reads.
6. Sam had to **pull** on his dog's leash to keep him away from the hornet's nest.

A	R	H	L	U	I
D	W	L	U	P	U
I	A	A	D	O	P
C	E	F	Y	N	U
R	O	U	N	D	
P		F	U	L	L

Word Box
away   round
pull   full
call   upon

20

Week 2

---

page 23

a–z

𝒜 ℬ 𝒞 𝒟 𝔼 𝔽
𝒢 ℋ ℐ 𝒥 𝒦 ℒ 𝑀
𝒩 𝒪 𝒫 𝒬 ℛ 𝒮 𝒯
𝒰 𝒱 𝒲 𝒳 𝒴 𝒵

Write.

Check your child's work.

23

---

page 24

Figure It Out

Read each sentence. Then color the numbered space in the picture that matches the number of the correct answer.

He rode his bike.
Who rode it?
1. a boy
2. a girl

Please bait my hook.
What am I doing?
7. fishing
8. playing baseball

Sorry! I broke it.
What could it be?
13. a stuffed animal
14. a crystal vase

Look at the dark cloud.
Where should you look?
19. down
20. up

The lamb lost its mother.
Who is its mother?
21. a sheep
22. a horse

She wore a red hat.
Who wore it?
23. a man
24. a woman

I see a thousand stars.
What time is it?
25. noon
26. night

Let's throw snowballs!
What time of year is it?
3. summer
4. winter

Breakfast is ready!
What time is it?
9. night
10. morning

He's a professor.
What is he?
15. an adult
16. a baby

Run, John, run!
What sport is John in?
5. swimming
6. track

I'm so thirsty.
What will I do?
11. drink something
12. eat something

It won't fit in the car.
What is it?
17. a football
18. a swing set

Riddle: What begins with T, ends with T, and has T in it? Find it in the puzzle.   **teapot**

24

---

page 25

Up the Elephant's Trunk

The elephant once said to me,
"Mouse, please climb in my nose
And go until I say to stop,
Then scratch there with your toes."

I climbed inside the long, deep trunk.
The air was damp and gray.
I walked across some peanut shells
And grass and bits of hay.

Then halfway up the bumpy trail
The elephant yelled, "Stop!"
"Scratch!" he said. "With all your might,
Just jump and kick and hop."

I scratched and itched and itched and scratched,
He finally yelled, "Enough!"
And then he blew me out his trunk
With lots of other stuff.

The elephant gave one big laugh
And said, "I thank you much."
And then he put his trunk on me
And gave me a warm touch.

SPECIAL WORDS
nose   long   trunk   damp   bumpy   trail

25

---

page 26

Up the Elephant's Trunk

Reading Comprehension

Fill in the blanks with the word that best completes the sentence.

1. The elephant said, "Mouse, please **climb** in my nose."
   walk   jump   climb   get

2. I walked across some peanut **shells**
   crumbs   shells   leaves   butter

3. Halfway up the bumpy **trail** the elephant yelled, "Stop!"
   road   path   street   trail

4. "Scratch!" he said. "With all your might, just jump and kick and **hop**
   hop   stomp   step   fall

5. He finally **yelled**, "Enough!"
   said   cried   yelled   shouted

Rhyme Time

Circle the words in each column that rhyme with the word in bold. What other words rhyme with that word? Write them on the lines below.

nose	**long**	**trunk**	**damp**	**bumpy**	**trail**
not	song	dunk	camp	lumpy	pail
goes	lone	sunk	ramp	humpy	sail
bows	wrong	truck	dump	puppy	tail

Answers will vary.

26

---

page 27

Grandma's Quilt

Solve the problems. If the answer is between 1 and 50, color the shape pink. If the answer is between 51 and 100, color the shape blue. Finish the design by coloring the other shapes with the colors of your choice.

45 −39 = 6
84 −59 = 25
71 −19 = 52
72 −55 = 17
60 −18 = 42
84 −26 = 59
74 −16 = 58
88 −29 = 59
98 −29 = 69
71 −17 = 54
82 −68 = 14
91 −32 = 59
92 −13 = 79
34 −16 = 18
43 −35 = 8
57 −28 = 29

Amelia bought 30 tickets for rides at the carnival. She used 15 tickets in the first hour. How many tickets did she have left?   **She had 15 tickets left.**

27

---

page 28

How to Agree

If the naming part of a sentence is a noun or pronoun that names one, the verb ends in **-s**, except for the pronouns I and **you**. If the naming part is a noun or pronoun that names more than one, the verb does not end in **-s**.

Read each sentence. Circle the correct verb to complete it.

1. John and his family (**camp**, camps) in the woods.
2. Alice (like, **likes**) hiking the best.
3. John (walk, **walks**) ahead of everyone.
4. Mom and John (**build**, builds) a campfire.
5. Dad and Alice (**cook**, cooks) dinner over the fire.
6. Alice and Mom (**crawl**, crawls) into the tent.

Choose two of the verbs you circled. Write a sentence using each verb.

Sentences will vary.

28

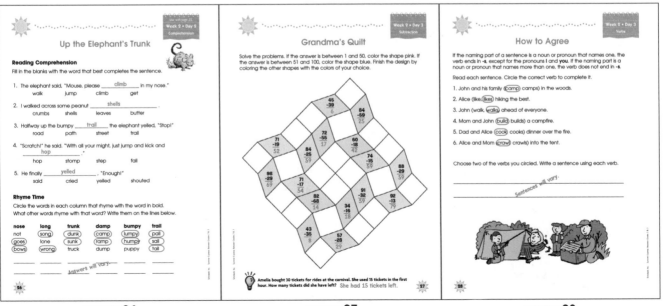

page 29

Draw a Picture

Verbs tell when action takes place. Present-tense verbs tell about action that is happening now. A verb showing the action of one person ends in **-s**. A verb telling the action of more than one person does not end in **-s**.

The boy sings.   The boys sing.

In the sentences below, underline each action verb. Then draw a picture that shows the action. Be sure to show if it is one person or animal doing the action or more than one person or animal doing the action.

1. Four birds <u>sit</u> on the fence.	2. That dog <u>digs</u>.
Check your child's work.	Check your child's work.

3. A man <u>sells</u> hotdogs.	4. The girls <u>run</u>.
Check your child's work.	Check your child's work.

Choose one of the pictures you drew. Write a short story about it.

page 30

Pick a Part

Circle the correct word to complete each sentence.

1. A leg is a part of a table, and a seat is a part of a ___chair___.
   A. rug   (B. chair)   C. bed

2. A string is a part of a harp, and a button is a part of a ___shirt___.
   (A. shirt)   B. snap   C. circle

3. A screen is a part of a TV, and a hand is a part of a ___clock___.
   A. broom   (B. clock)   C. knob

4. A yolk is a part of an egg, and a pit is a part of a ___peach___.
   (A. peach)   B. hen   C. word

5. A heel is a part of a foot, and an eye is a part of a ___face___.
   A. toe   B. nose   (C. face)

6. A stove is a part of a kitchen, and a couch is a part of a ___den___.
   (A. den)   B. sink   C. floor

7. A wing is a part of a bird, and a sleeve is a part of a ___sweater___.
   A. nest   (B. sweater)   C. pocket

8. A drawer is a part of a desk, and a pedal is a part of a ___bike___.
   A. ladder   B. step   (C. bike)

Name two things that each of these can be a part of: ear, eye, arm, leg, and neck.
Answers will vary.

page 31

Tricky Twins

Sandy and Mandy are having a twin party. There are six sets of twins, but only one set of identical twins. To find the identical twins, solve the addition problems under each person. The identical twins have the same answer.

207 + 434 = 641	126 + 89 = 215	328 + 367 = 695	257 + 568 = 825
547 + 129 = 676	**624 + 127 = 751**	**108 + 107 = 215**	**229 + 337 = 566**
258 + 378 = 636	379 + 336 = 715	417 + 109 = 526	153 + 494 = 647

page 32

Seashore Sentences

Complete:
A ___statement___ ends with a period.
A ___question___ ends with a question mark.
An ___exclamation___ ends with an exclamation point.

Write a statement (S), a question (Q), and an exclamation (E) about each picture.

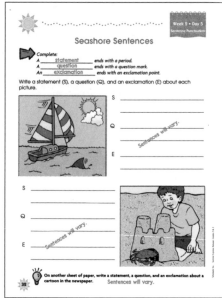

S _____
Q _____   *Sentences will vary.*
E _____

S _____
Q _____   *Sentences will vary.*
E _____

On another sheet of paper, write a statement, a question, and an exclamation about a cartoon in the newspaper.
Sentences will vary.

Week 3

page 35

a-z
a b c d e f g
h i j k l m
n o p q r s t
u v w x y z

Write.

_____
Check your child's work.
_____

page 36

Describe a Noun

An **adjective** describes a person, place, or thing. Color, size, and number words are adjectives.

Read each sentence. Find the adjective and the noun it describes. Circle the noun. Write the adjective on the line.

1. Peggy and Rosa went to the big (zoo).   big

2. They looked up at the tall (giraffe).   tall

3. The giraffe looked down at the two (girls).   two

4. The giraffe had brown (spots).   brown

Write adjectives from the sentences in the chart.

Color Word	Size Words	Number Word
brown	big	two
	tall	

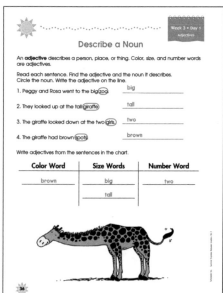

page 37

Panda Pair

In 1972, Americans fell in love with two giant pandas named Hsing-Hsing and Ling-Ling. The pandas came to the United States from China. The National Zoo in Washington, D.C., became the pandas' new home. On their first day there, 20,000 people visited the two pandas. The crowds kept coming year after year.

Hsing-Hsing and Ling-Ling were just cubs when they got to the United States. As the years passed, many hoped the pair would have cubs of their own. Ling-Ling gave birth several times. But none of the babies lived more than a few days. Each time a cub died, people around the world felt sad.

Both pandas lived to an old age. Ling-Ling was 23 when she died in 1992. Hsing-Hsing died in 1999 at the age of 28. But the pandas were not forgotten. At the National Zoo, the glass walls of their home were covered with letters from children. The letters expressed the children's love for the pandas and told how much they were missed.

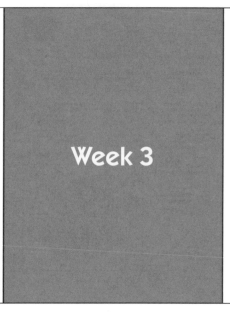

1. **The author wrote this passage mostly to:**
   (A. tell about Hsing-Hsing and Ling-Ling.)
   B. explain where giant pandas come from.
   C. describe a giant panda's cubs.
   D. convince people to visit the National Zoo.

2. **According to the author, how did people feel about the pandas?**
   Answers will vary.

3. **If you visited the National Zoo in 2000, what would you have seen at the pandas' home?**
   Answers will vary.

page 38

Number Words

Write each sentence using numbers and symbols.

Cats aren't supposed to count!   one, two, three...

1. Four plus five is nine.	4 + 5 = 9
2. Eleven minus six is five.	11 − 6 = 5
3. Nine plus seven is sixteen.	9 + 7 = 16
4. Four plus eight is twelve.	4 + 8 = 12
5. Three minus two is one.	3 − 2 = 1
6. Seven plus seven is fourteen.	7 + 7 = 14
7. Fifteen minus ten is five.	15 − 10 = 5
8. Two plus eight is ten.	2 + 8 = 10
9. Five minus two is three.	5 − 2 = 3

page 39

Who Is Speaking?

Quotation marks show the exact words someone says. They go before the speaker's first word. They also go after the speaker's last word and the end punctuation mark.

Read each sentence. Underline the exact words the speaker says. Put the words in quotation marks. The first one is done for you.

1. Max said, "Let's go on a picnic."

2. Cori replied, "That's a great idea."

3. Andy asked, "What should we bring?"

4. Max said with a laugh, "We should bring food."

5. Cori added, "Yes, let's bring lots and lots of food."

6. Andy giggled and said, "You're no help at all!"

Finish the sentences below by writing what Max, Cori, and Andy might say next. Use quotation marks.

7. Max said, _____

8. Cori asked, _____

9. Andy answered, _____

Sentences will vary.

39

page 40

Same As. . .

Circle the correct word to complete each sentence.

1. A stick is like a stake, and a cap is like a _____.
   A. sock   B. hat   C. twig

2. A runner is like a racer, and a smile is like a _____.
   A. frown   B. face   C. grin

3. A crowd is like a mob, and a song is like a _____.
   A. group   B. tune   C. flute

4. A dinner is like a supper, and a pot is like a _____.
   A. pan   B. cook   C. meal

5. Fur is like fuzz, and wet is like _____.
   A. messy   B. dry   C. damp

6. Sad is like gloomy, and happy is like _____.
   A. glad   B. mad   C. nice

7. Misty is like foggy, and fast is like _____.
   A. runner   B. quick   C. slow

8. Look is like see, and sleep is like _____.
   A. nap   B. wake   C. find

Discuss with someone in your family why you did not choose the other words.

40

page 41

Sandwich Shop

Menu

hot dog $1.53	fruit salad..........$1.90
pbj $1.49	veggies & dip $1.84
turkey sub..........$1.86	chips ....$ .50
hamburger..........$1.72	fries ....$ .65
juice ....$ .84	cupcake..........$1.07
milk ....$ .75	brownie $1.22
shake $1.17	cookies ....$ .86

Add.

A.
pbj $1.49
chips $.50
milk $.75
brownie + $1.22
          $3.96

B.
hamburger $1.72
fries $.65
shake   + $1.17
          $3.54

C.
turkey sub $1.86
veggies &
dip $1.84
juice $.84
cupcake + $1.07
           $5.61

D.
hot dog $1.53
fruit salad $1.90
brownie $1.22
juice   + $.84
            $5.49

E.
turkey sub $1.86
chips $.50
shake   + $1.17
           $3.53

F.
pbj $1.49
cookies $.86
milk   + $.75
           $3.10

41

page 42

Celebrating Our Country

Draw a picture of something you do to celebrate the Fourth of July.

Answers will vary.

Word Bank
eat
play
swim
fireworks
cookout
picnic
beach
park
country
history
family
free
proud
happy

On the Fourth of July, I _____

I celebrate this holiday with _____ *Answers will vary.*

On the Fourth of July, I also like to _____

We celebrate this holiday because _____ *Answers will vary.*

42

page 43

Sort It Out!

Put each word from the Word Box in the circle where it belongs. We did the first one for you.

Word Box
found   find   behind
away   upon   pull
call   put   above
below   around

Action Words
found
call
find
put
pull

Direction Words
away
below
upon
around
behind
above

Now try this!
Write a sentence using as many words from the Word Box as you can.

_____ *Answers will vary.*

How many words from the Word Box did you use? _____

43

page 44

Fancy Fireworks

Kaboom! It's the Fourth of July. Fireworks light up the night. Have you ever seen a willow firework? It has long trails of color that float to the ground. The pinwheel and comet are two other popular fireworks. One of the loudest fireworks is called the salute. After a bright flash, you hear a loud BOOM!

Read the paragraph. Then answer the questions.

1. Which firework has long trails of color? __willow__

2. Which firework makes a loud BOOM? __salute__

3. What is a popular firework? __pinwheel or comet__

Add three more details to the web.

Answers will vary.

pinwheel
detail

Kinds of Fireworks

topic

MORE! What do you think a pinwheel firework looks like? Draw a picture to show your ideas.

44

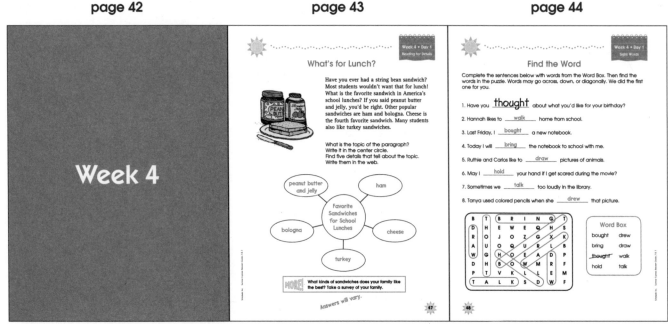

Week 4

page 47

What's for Lunch?

Have you ever had a string bean sandwich? Most students wouldn't want that for lunch! What is the favorite sandwich in America's school lunches? If you said peanut butter and jelly, you'd be right. Other popular sandwiches are ham and bologna. Cheese is the fourth favorite sandwich. Many students also like turkey sandwiches.

What is the topic of the paragraph? Write it in the center circle. Find five details that tell about the topic. Write them in the web.

Favorite Sandwiches for School Lunches
peanut butter and jelly
ham
bologna
cheese
turkey

MORE! What kinds of sandwiches does your family like the best? Take a survey of your family.

Answers will vary.

47

page 48

Find the Word

Complete the sentences below with words from the Word Box. Then find the words in the puzzle. Words may go across, down, or diagonally. We did the first one for you.

1. Have you __thought__ about what you'd like for your birthday?

2. Hannah likes to __walk__ home from school.

3. Last Friday, I __bought__ a new notebook.

4. Today I will __bring__ the notebook to school with me.

5. Ruthie and Carlos like to __draw__ pictures of animals.

6. May I __hold__ your hand if I get scared during the movie?

7. Sometimes we __talk__ too loudly in the library.

8. Tanya used colored pencils when she __drew__ that picture.

Word Box
bought   drew
bring   draw
~~thought~~   walk
hold   talk

48

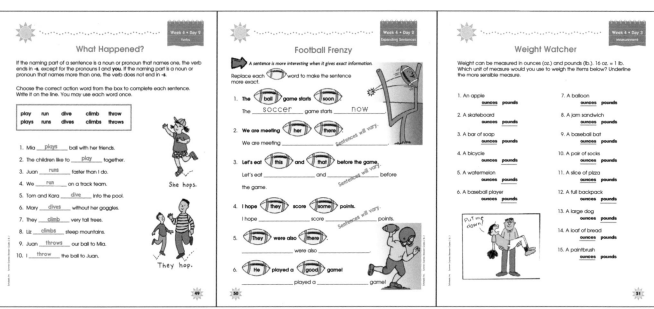

page 49

What Happened?

If the naming part of a sentence is a noun or pronoun that names one, the verb ends in -s, except for the pronouns I and you. If the naming part is a noun or pronoun that names more than one, the verb does not end in -s.

Choose the correct action word from the box to complete each sentence. Write it on the line. You may use each word once.

| play | run | dive | climb | throw |
| plays | runs | dives | climbs | throws |

1. Mia __plays__ ball with her friends.
2. The children like to __play__ together.
3. Juan __runs__ faster than I do.
4. We __run__ on a track team.
5. Tom and Kara __dive__ into the pool.
6. Mary __dives__ without her goggles.
7. They __climb__ very tall trees.
8. Liz __climbs__ steep mountains.
9. Juan __throws__ our ball to Mia.
10. I __throw__ the ball to Juan.

She hops.

They hop.

page 50

Football Frenzy

A sentence is more interesting when it gives exact information.

Replace each 🏈 word to make the sentence more exact.

1. The (ball) game starts (soon).
   The __soccer__ game starts __now__.
2. We are meeting (her) (there).
   We are meeting _____ Sentences will vary.
3. Let's eat (this) and (that) before the game.
   Let's eat _____ and _____ before the game. Sentences will vary.
4. I hope (they) score (some) points.
   I hope _____ score _____ points. Sentences will vary.
5. (They) were also (there).
   _____ were also _____ Sentences will vary.
6. (He) played a (good) game!
   _____ played a _____ game!

page 51

Weight Watcher

Weight can be measured in ounces (oz.) and pounds (lb.). 16 oz. = 1 lb. Which unit of measure would you use to weigh the items below? Underline the more sensible measure.

1. An apple — ounces **pounds**
2. A skateboard — ounces **pounds**
3. A bar of soap — **ounces** pounds
4. A bicycle — ounces **pounds**
5. A watermelon — ounces **pounds**
6. A baseball player — ounces **pounds**
7. A balloon — **ounces** pounds
8. A jam sandwich — **ounces** pounds
9. A baseball bat — ounces **pounds**
10. A pair of socks — **ounces** pounds
11. A slice of pizza — **ounces** pounds
12. A full backpack — ounces **pounds**
13. A large dog — ounces **pounds**
14. A loaf of bread — ounces **pounds**
15. A paintbrush — **ounces** pounds

Put me down!

page 52

Lost and Found

Read the story. Then fill in the bubble next to the best answer to each question below.

One day Alisha's little brother found **three** dollars. "Look!" he said. "Now I can buy a pony!"
"I think a pony will cost too **much**," Alisha said. "**Shall** I help you **find** something to spend it on?"
"Okay," he said. He **put** the money in his pocket.
"Ice cream might be a good thing to spend it on," said Alisha.
"What **kind** do you want?"
"I **only** like one kind. Chocolate," said her brother.
"I think chocolate is the best kind, **too**," said Alisha.

1. When Alisha says a pony will cost too **much**, she means
   ○ a. Three dollars is more than enough money to buy a pony.
   ● b. A pony costs a lot more than three dollars.
   ○ c. If her brother had found three dollars, he could buy a pony.

2. When Alisha says, "I think chocolate is the best kind, **too**," the word **too** means
   ● a. also.
   ○ b. two.
   ○ c. not at all.

3. The opposite of **found** is
   ○ a. kept.
   ○ b. forgot.
   ● c. lost.

4. Which word means the same as **kind** in this story?
   ○ a. nice
   ○ b. child
   ● c. type

5. In the dictionary, the word **only** appears
   ● a. between the words **lonely** and **quiet**.
   ○ b. after the word **totally**.
   ○ c. before the word **night**.

page 53

Letter From Vera

April 11

Dear Morey,
I just got your letter with the picture of you riding your bike. From the smile on your face, I can tell how much fun you're having. I still remember when you could hardly ride a tricycle. You've come a long way!
Now here's some advice. I'm sure you're a good rider. But you will fall off your bike now and then. So please get yourself a helmet. Wear it every time you ride. A helmet will help protect you from a head injury. Wearing a helmet when you ride a bike is as important as wearing your seat belt when you ride in a car!
No, I'm not trying to be a bossy know-it-all. I just don't want a bad fall to wipe that smile off your face. When you come to visit this summer, bring your bike and your helmet. We'll take some great rides together!

Your cousin,
Vera

1. From this letter, what can you tell about the picture of Morey that he sent to Vera?
   A. He is riding a tricycle.
   B. He is not wearing a helmet.
   C. He is in his driveway.
   D. He is looking scared.

2. Vera's advice shows that she:
   F. cares a lot about safety.
   G. is often bossy and mean.
   H. doesn't like riding bikes.
   J. is learning to drive a car.

3. What will Morey do with Vera during the summer?
   _____ Answers will vary. _____

page 54

A Verb Puzzle

Verbs tell when action takes place. Past-tense verbs tell about action that happened in the past. Most past-tense verbs end in **-ed**.

Write the past tense of each verb in the box. Then use the past tense words to complete the puzzle below.

call	called	mix	mixed	play	played
yell	yelled	kick	kicked	help	helped
bark	barked	climb	climbed	walk	walked

Across
1. Mike __climbed__ over the wall.
3. The dog __barked__.
5. Our teacher __helped__ us with the math problems.
7. We __yelled__ at the team to win.
8. The boys __walked__ home from school.

Down
2. Sam __called__ his dad on the phone.
2. Grandma __mixed__ the cake batter.
4. The player __kicked__ the ball.
6. Marie __played__ a game with Zack.

Write a sentence using each of the verbs from the puzzle.
Answers will vary.

page 55

How Many Legs?

Fill in the blanks.

1. How many legs on
   1 turkey __2__ 3 turkeys __6__
   2 turkeys __4__ 4 turkeys __8__

2. How many legs on
   1 cat __4__ 3 cats __12__
   2 cats __8__ 4 cats __16__

3. How many legs on
   1 ladybug __6__ 3 ladybugs __18__
   2 ladybugs __12__ 4 ladybugs __24__

4. How many legs on
   1 spider __8__ 3 spiders __24__
   2 spiders __16__ 4 spiders __32__

5. How many legs on
   1 squid __10__ 6 squid __60__
   2 squid __20__ 7 squid __70__
   3 squid __30__ 8 squid __80__
   4 squid __40__ 9 squid __90__
   5 squid __50__ 10 squid __100__

page 56

Mystery Bags

Adjectives are words that help you imagine how something looks, feels, smells, sounds, or tastes.

Make a list of words that describe the object in each bag below.

List of words will vary.

List of words will vary.

Use a paper sack to make a real mystery bag. Place an object in the bag and give describing clues to someone. Can he or she guess the mystery object?

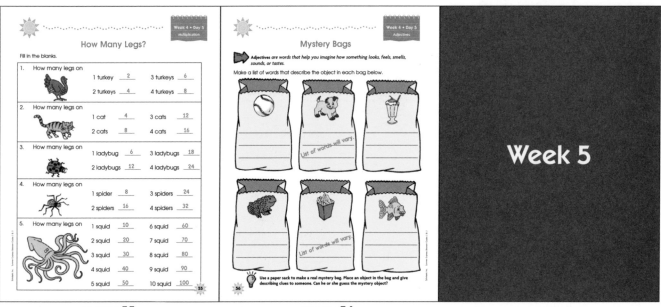

Week 5

page 59

Foreign Flags

Every country has its own flag. Japan has a white flag with a red circle on it. The red circle stands for the sun. Japan's name means the "land of the rising sun." Canada also has a red and white flag. But its flag has a white background with two wide red stripes. In the center of the flag is a red maple leaf. The maple tree is a symbol of Canada.

Read the paragraph. Then answer the questions.

1. What colors are both flags? red and white
2. What does Japan's flag have in the center? red circle for sun
3. What does Canada's flag have in the center? red maple leaf
4. How are the backgrounds of the two flags different?
Japan: white background; Canada: white background with 2 red stripes

Write your answers in the correct parts of the circles.

Japan — red circle for sun, white background
Both — red and white
Canada — red maple leaf, white background with 2 red stripes

MORE! Find Japan and Canada on a world map.

59

---

page 60

Verb *to be*

Am, is, are, was, and **were** are forms of the verb **to be**. These verbs show being instead of action.

Read each sentence. Underline the verb. Write **past** if the sentence tells about the past. Write **now** if the sentence tells about the present.

1. The story is perfect. ___ now
2. The producers are happy. ___ now
3. The actors were funny. ___ past
4. The movie studio is interested in the story. ___ now
5. I am excited about the movie. ___ now
6. I was sad at the end. ___ past

60

---

page 61

Numbers 0-9

Trace and write.

0
1
2
3
Check your child's writing.
4
5
6
7
8
9

61

---

page 62

Field Trip Cars

1. Josie's class is going to the teddy bear factory.
Three children will ride in each car.
Draw a circle around the children who will ride in each car.

How many cars do they need? 3

2. Pete's class is going to see the elephant seals.
Five children will ride in each van.
Draw a circle around the children who will ride in each van.

How many vans do they need? 3

3. Rosa's class is going to the Space Museum.
Eight children will ride in each small bus.
Draw a circle around the children who will ride in each bus.

How many small buses do they need? 2

62

---

page 63

Contractions With *not*

A **contraction** is two words made into one word. An **apostrophe** takes the place of the missing letter or letters. In a contraction, **not** becomes **n't**.

Read each sentence. Write a contraction for the underlined words.

1. Cindy and Ed could not bake a cake. couldn't
2. There was not enough flour. wasn't
3. They are not happy. aren't
4. Do not give up! don't
5. They did not give up.
They made cupcakes! didn't

Write a sentence using a contraction you wrote.

Sentences will vary.

63

---

page 64

Chilly or Chili?

Homophones are words that sound the same but are spelled differently and have different meanings.

Write the correct homophone in each blank to complete the sentences.

1. bored, board
Some of the board members seemed quite bored at the last meeting.

2. bare, bear
When a bear cub is born, it is bare and its eyes are closed.

3. chilly, chili
Nothing tastes better than a bowl of chili on a chilly day.

4. guest, guessed
Who would have guessed that your guest was a thief!

5. patients, patience
I wonder if doctors ever lose their patience with difficult patients.

On another sheet of paper, rewrite each sentence using the correct homophones.

6. I'll meet you at ate inn the mourning.
I'll meet you at eight in the morning.

7. Would ewe fix me sum tee and a bowl of serial?
Would you fix me some tea and a bowl of cereal?

8. My ant and uncle lived oversees four too years in Madrid.
My aunt and uncle lived overseas for two years in Madrid.

9. Alex was sick with the flue and mist a hole weak of school.
Alex was sick with the flu and missed a whole week of school.

10. I want two bye a knew pear of shoes, but I dew knot have a sent left.
I want to buy a new pair of shoes, but I do not have a cent left.

64

---

page 65

A State Apart

The state of Michigan has two parts—the Upper Peninsula and the Lower Peninsula. Peninsulas are long arms of land that jut into water. Both of Michigan's peninsulas are almost surrounded by the Great Lakes. The Upper Peninsula has many big forests. It is also rich in minerals. The Lower Peninsula has more people and large cities. Most of the state's industry is in the Lower Peninsula. Both peninsulas attract tourists who come to spend vacations in Michigan.

Read the paragraph. Add headings to the Venn diagram. Then write facts in each part of the diagram.

Upper Peninsula — big forests, rich in minerals
Both — attract tourists, part of Michigan, surrounded by Great Lakes
Lower Peninsula — more people and large cities, most of industry, larger in area

MORE! The Lower Peninsula of Michigan is larger in area than the Upper Peninsula. Add this fact to the diagram.

65

---

page 66

Garage Sale

Find and mark the ten spelling errors.

great
We have grate stuff and big bargains!

Supplies
Office Supplys
• Big boxes of old newspaper
• Ballpoint pens that are out of ink
• Broken rubber bands
• Empty printer ink containers

Clothing
• Single left shoes
• Socks with holes
• Jackets with broken zippers
• Sleeves that were cut off a shirt

Household Goods
• Old phone books
• Torn sheets
• Old toothbrushes
• Empty paint cans
• Chipped plates
• A bunch of old pizza boxes

Furniture and Hardware
• A big box of bent nails
• A saggy bed
• A sofa with mice living in it
• A chair with only three legs
• A TV with only one channel
• Old door knobs

66

---

page 67

Cow Code

Riddle: Where do cows go for entertainment?

Decoder
23 X
17 .... O
153 .... E
21 .... A
370 .... O
108 .... S
76 .... D
9 V
15 .... F
67 .... T
22 .... E
435 .... P
86 .... H
88 .... R
45 I
534 .... M
118 .... W
543 .... N
307 .... G

What to Do
Find the corresponding numerals below. Then use the Decoder to solve the riddle by filling in the spaces at the bottom of the page. The first one has been done for you.

1. nine — 9
2. twenty-two — 22
3. seventeen — 17
4. forty-five — 45
5. sixty-seven — 67
6. one hundred eight — 108
7. eighty-six — 86
8. one hundred fifty-three — 153
9. three hundred seventy — 370
10. five hundred thirty-four — 534

TO t h e " m o o " v i e s
    5 7 2 10 3 9 1 4 8 6

67

page 68

Week 5 • Day 5
Combining Sentences

Cake and Ice Cream

Two sentences that share the same subject can be combined to make one sentence by using the word *and*.

Rewrite the sentences by combining their endings.

1. The party was fun.
The party was exciting.
The party was fun and exciting.

2. We blew up orange balloons.
We blew up red balloons.
We blew up orange and red balloons.

3. We ate cake.
We ate ice cream.
We ate cake and ice cream.

4. The cake frosting was green.
The cake frosting was yellow.
The cake frosting was green and yellow.

5. We made a bookmark.
We made a clay pot.
We made a bookmark and a clay pot.

6. We brought games.
We brought prizes.
We brought games and prizes.

68

page 68

Week 6

Week 6

page 71

Use with page 72.
Week 6 • Day 1
Comprehension

Cleaning the Alligator's Teeth

The alligator asked if I
Would clean his dirty teeth.
I climbed inside his jagged jaws
And brushed up underneath.

I felt his two jaws start to close.
His sharp teeth touched my skin.
I yelled, "I'm not a sandwich!
Open up and give a grin!"

The alligator laughed and made
His two jaws open wide.
I said, "The next time you do that
I'll have to pinch your hide."

He gave another 'gator laugh
That shook me head to toe.
I finished brushing all his teeth
And said, "I've got to go."

SPECIAL WORDS
clean   jaws   start   grin   wide   stood

71

page 71

page 72

Use with page 71.
Week 6 • Day 1
Comprehension

Cleaning the Alligator's Teeth

Reading Comprehension
Fill in the blanks with the word that best completes the sentence.

1. The alligator asked if I would clean his dirty _____teeth_____.
claws   teeth   scales   tail

2. I climbed inside his jagged _____jaws_____
nose   ears   mouth   jaws

3. I felt his two jaws start to _____close_____.
open   chew   lick   close

4. His _____sharp_____ teeth touched my skin.
many   white   sharp   mean

5. I yelled, "I'm not a sandwich! Open up and give a _____grin_____!"
laugh   grin   yell   bite

Rhyme Time
Circle the words in each column that rhyme with the word in bold. What other words rhyme with that word? Write them on the lines below.

clean	jaws	start	grin	wide	stood
(bean)	(claws)	(dart)	(win)	wind	(good)
(mean)	jam	star	(fin)	(hide)	stop
(seen)	(laws)	(cart)	(pin)	(ride)	(hood)

_____ Answers will vary. _____

72

page 72

page 73

Week 5 • Day 2
Place Value

Colorful Fish

Look at the numbers in the shapes inside the fish.

Use the information in the key at right to color the shapes.

If there is a . . .	Color the space . . .
6 in the tens place	green
5 in the hundreds place	blue
2 in the ones place	yellow
7 in the tens place	orange
9 in the hundreds place	red

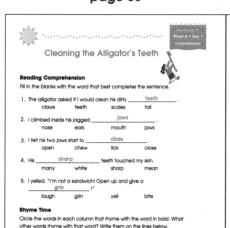

1.

2.

3.

4.

5.

6.

7.

73

page 73

page 74

Week 6 • Day 2
Verbs

Verbs *have*, *had*

The verb **to have** is irregular. Use **have** or **has** to tell about the present. Use **had** to tell about the past.

Choose the correct word from the chart to complete each sentence.

In the Present	In the Past
have, has	had

1. Joe _____has_____ new running shoes.

2. I _____have_____ new shoes, too.

3. Last week we _____had_____ old shoes.

4. I _____have_____ a green shirt on.

5. Joe _____has_____ a blue shirt on.

6. Yesterday we both _____had_____ red shirts on.

7. Last year we _____had_____ to walk to the park.

8. Now, I _____have_____ skates.

9. Now Joe _____has_____ a bike.

74

page 74

page 75

Week 6 • Day 3
Building Sentences

Get Your Ticket!

Write a sentence to match each picture. Be sure to include a subject, an action, and a part that tells where or when.

1. **A boy climbs a tree in his backyard.**

2. Answers will vary.

3. Answers will vary.

Find a cartoon in the newspaper. Use the pictures to write a sentence on another sheet of paper. Be sure to include a subject, an action, and a part that tells where or when.

75

page 75

page 76

Week 6 • Day 3
Building Sentences

Slide Show

A sentence is more interesting when it includes a subject, an action, and a part that tells where or when.

Write three sentences and draw pictures to match.

subject	action	where or when
	Answers will vary.	

1. _____

subject	action	where or when
	Answers will vary.	

2. _____

subject	action	where or when
	Answers will vary.	

3. _____

Switch the sentence parts around to make three silly sentences! Write the sentences on another sheet of paper.

76

page 76

page 77

Week 6 • Day 4
Comprehension

Play Ball

What's your favorite ball game? Many people like sports in which they throw a ball. In bowling and basketball, you throw a ball. Other people play games in which they hit a ball. Golf and tennis are two examples. Still another game in which a ball is hit is lacrosse. A third kind of ball game calls for kicking a ball. Players kick balls in soccer, football, rugby, and of course, kickball.

Read the paragraph. Then answer the questions.

1. What are four sports where you kick a ball? soccer, football, rugby, kickball

2. What are three sports in which you hit a ball? golf, tennis, lacrosse

3. In what games do you throw a ball? basketball, bowling

Use your answers to complete the chart.

Hitting a Ball	Throwing a Ball	Kicking a Ball
golf	basketball	soccer
tennis	bowling	football
lacrosse	baseball	rugby
baseball		kickball

MORE   What do you do with the ball in baseball? Add baseball to the chart.

77

page 77

page 78

Send In the Subs

A **pronoun** is a word that can take the place of a noun.

The nouns in these sentences need a rest. Pick a pronoun to replace the underlined word(s). Then write the sentence with the pronoun.

Pronoun Subs					
he	you	we	they	it	she

1. <u>Tanya</u> swings the bat.
   She swings the bat.

2. <u>Mr. Bartlet and Mr. Jones</u> blow their whistles.
   They blow their whistles.

3. <u>Matt and I</u> warm up.
   We warm up.

4. <u>Leo</u> looks for his glove.
   He looks for his glove.

5. <u>The ball</u> rolls into the field.
   It rolls into the field.

Check your sentences. Did you begin them with a capital letter?

78

page 79

Prime Timer

Write the time 3 ways.

example: 1:15
15 minutes after 1
45 minutes to 2

1.   7:35
35 minutes after 7
25 minutes to 8

2.   3:50
50 minutes after 3
10 minutes to 4

3.   9:15
15 minutes after 9
45 minutes to 10

4.   6:25
25 minutes after 6
35 minutes to 7

5.   9:55
55 minutes after 9
5 minutes to 10

6.   2:05
5 minutes after 2
55 minutes to 3

79

page 80

Describing a Surprise

Use adjectives to describe an object.

Read the words on the box.
What do they describe?

clouds

white	high
puffy	moving

Think of a surprise to hide in each box. Then write four adjectives to describe it.

1. Answers will vary.
2. Answers will vary.
3. Answers will vary.
4. Answers will vary.

Read your adjectives to a friend. Can your friend guess what the surprise is? If not, can you think of better adjectives?

80

Week 7

page 83

Fraction Fun

Something that is split in 2 equal parts is divided in "half."

These two shapes are divided in half.

A fraction has a number on the top: → 1
A fraction has a number on the bottom, too: → 2
The top number tells the "fraction," or parts, of the whole.
The bottom number tells the number of parts in the whole.

A. Draw a line to match the picture with a fraction.

$\frac{2}{2}$ $\frac{2}{12}$ $\frac{2}{3}$

B. The top number in these fractions tells you how many parts to color. Try it!

color $\frac{1}{2}$ color $\frac{2}{2}$

83

page 84

Statements and Questions

A **statement** is a sentence that tells something. It ends with a period.
A **question** is a sentence that asks something. It ends with a question mark.

A. Read each sentence. Write Q on the line if the sentence is a question. Write S if the sentence is a statement.

1. Where did the ant live?   Q
2. The ant had many cousins.   S
3. She found the crumb under a leaf.   S
4. How will she carry it?   Q
5. Who came along first?   Q
6. The lizard wouldn't help.   S
7. He said he was too cold.   S
8. Why did the rooster fly away?   Q

B. The sentences below do not make sense. Rewrite the words in the correct order.

1. How crumb did carry the ant the?
   How did the ant carry the crumb?

2. She herself it carried.
   She carried it herself.

84

page 85

Blending In

How are the following words alike: *blue, black, blink*? If you said they all begin with *bl*, you're right. Some other words that begin with these letters are *blob, blanket,* and *blimp*. Letter pairs like *bl* are "blends." Blends are two or more consonants that work together. What blend do the following words begin with: *green, gray, grumpy*? Two other blends are *tr* and *sm*. Words such as *smoke, smile, try, tray, smack, trick, truck,* and *smell* begin with these blends.

Use the paragraph to write four headings for the chart. Then write examples under each heading.

BL	GR	TR	SM
blue	green	try	smoke
black	gray	tray	smile
blink	grumpy	trick	smack
blob		truck	smell
blanket			
blimp			

MORE! Add at least two more words to each group on the chart.

85

page 86

Great Gardening Tips

Sentences can also be combined to make them more interesting. Key words can help put two sentences together.

old: I will plan my garden. I am waiting for spring.
new: I will plan my garden while I am waiting for spring.

Write a new sentence using the key word in each flower.

1. Fill a cup with water. Add some flower seeds.   *and*
   Fill a cup with water and add some flower seeds.

2. This will soften the seeds. They are hard.   *because*
   This will soften the seeds because they are hard.

3. Fill a cup with dirt. The seeds soak in water.   *while*
   Fill a cup with dirt while the seeds soak in water.

4. Bury the seeds in the cup. The dirt covers them.   *until*
   Bury the seeds in the cup until the dirt covers them.

5. Add water to the plant. Do not add too much.   *but*
   Add water to the plant but do not add too much.

6. Set the cup in the sun. The plant will grow.   *so*
   Set the cup in the sun so the plant will grow.

86

page 87

A-maze-ing Verbs

To complete the maze, pass only through the correct sentences. An incorrect sentence is like a wall in the maze: You cannot pass through it. The correct path takes you through nine boxes.

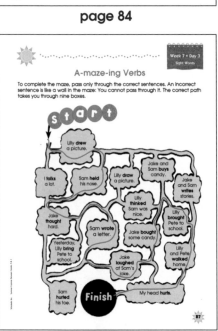

start

Lilly drew a picture.

I talks a lot.

Sam held his nose.

Lilly draw a picture.

Jake and Sam buys candy.

Jake and Sam writes stories.

Lilly thinked Sam was nice.

Lilly brought Pete to school.

Jake thought hard.

Sam wrote a letter.

Jake bought some candy.

Yesterday, Lilly bring Pete to school.

Jake laughed at Sam's joke.

Lilly and Pete walked home.

Sam hurted his toe.

Finish

My head hurts.

page 88

Three Nests

You can use **adjectives** to compare things. To compare two things, add -er to the adjective. To compare three or more things, add -est.

Biddie Bird has a friend named Betty. Betty always wants to outdo Biddie. If Biddie has a clean nest, Betty has a cleaner nest. Biddie and Betty have another friend named Birdie. She likes to outdo both Biddie and Betty. So she has the cleanest nest.

Read the sentences. Then fill in the chart so the correct form of each adjective is under each bird's name.

	Biddie	Betty	Birdie
	clean	cleaner	cleanest
1.	new	newer	newest
2.	small	smaller	smallest
3.	warm	warmer	warmest
4.	round	rounder	roundest
5.	neat	neater	neatest
6.	soft	softer	softest

1. Betty's nest is <u>newer</u> than Biddie's.

2. Biddie has a <u>small</u> nest.

3. Birdie has the <u>warmest</u> nest of all.

4. Biddie's nest is <u>round</u>.

5. Birdie built the <u>neatest</u> nest.

6. Betty has a <u>softer</u> nest than Biddie.

On another sheet of paper, use the words you wrote on the chart to draw a picture of each bird's nest.

88

page 89

Fool the Birds

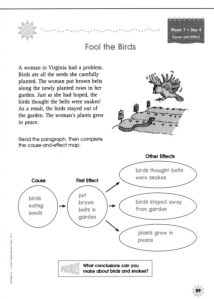

A woman in Virginia had a problem. Birds ate all the seeds she carefully planted. The woman put brown belts along the newly planted rows in her garden. Just as she had hoped, the birds thought the belts were snakes! As a result, the birds stayed out of the garden. The woman's plants grew in peace.

Read the paragraph. Then complete the cause-and-effect map.

Other Effects

Cause
birds eating seeds

First Effect
put brown belts in garden

→ birds thought belts were snakes

→ birds stayed away from garden

→ plants grew in peace

MORE! What conclusions can you make about birds and snakes?

89

page 90

Banana-Rama

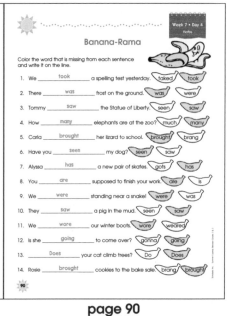

Color the word that is missing from each sentence and write it on the line.

1. We <u>took</u> a spelling test yesterday. taked / took

2. There <u>was</u> frost on the ground. was / were

3. Tommy <u>saw</u> the Statue of Liberty. seen / saw

4. How <u>many</u> elephants are at the zoo? much / many

5. Carla <u>brought</u> her lizard to school. brought / brang

6. Have you <u>seen</u> my dog? seen / saw

7. Alyssa <u>has</u> a new pair of skates. gots / has

8. You <u>are</u> supposed to finish your work. are / is

9. We <u>were</u> standing near a snake! were / was

10. They <u>saw</u> a pig in the mud. seen / saw

11. We <u>wore</u> our winter boots. wore / weared

12. Is she <u>going</u> to come over? gonna / going

13. <u>Does</u> your cat climb trees? Do / Does

14. Rosie <u>brought</u> cookies to the bake sale. brang / brought

90

page 91

A Ray of Fun

An **array** demonstrates a multiplication sentence. The first **factor** tells how many rows there are. The second **factor** tells how many there are in each row. The answer of a multiplication sentence is called the **product**.

2 × 4 = 8   2 rows
4 in each row

Write the multiplication sentence for each array.

A. 2 × 3 = 6

B. 3 × 3 = 9

C. 4 × 2 = 8

D. 3 × 5 = 15

E. 1 × 3 = 3

F. 4 × 3 = 12

G. 2 × 6 = 12

H. 3 × 4 = 12

I. 3 × 6 = 18

J. 5 × 3 = 15

K. 5 × 1 = 5

L. 7 × 2 = 14

It was time for our family photo. The photographer arranged us into four rows. There were six people in each row. How many people in all were in the photo? On another sheet of paper, draw an array to solve this problem. **24 people. Check array.**

91

page 92

How Unusual!

The prefix **un-** means either "not" or "do the opposite of" the base word. Circle each base word in the puzzle. The words go , , and . We did the first one for you.

unpack	untie	unload	unlock	unwind	undo
unknown	unfold	unable	unfair	unusual	unwise

R	A	I	L	I	M	A	F	X
N	E	E	O	F	F	O	L	D
A	I	W	A	E	A	X	L	E
T	S	X	D	L	I	I	O	T
R	E	V	O	C	Z	R	D	N
U	P	A	C	K	E	B	W	Y
C	A	B	L	E	S	Y	Z	P
D	N	I	K	U	S	U	A	L

Write a word from the list to complete each sentence.

1. It is <u>unusual</u> for James to be late for school.

2. It took me ten minutes to <u>untie</u> the knot.

3. You need a key to <u>unlock</u> the trunk.

4. We grew more concerned as the story began to <u>unfold</u>.

5. It is <u>unwise</u> to wait until the last minute to do your homework.

6. Bill thought the umpire's call was <u>unfair</u>.

92

Week 8

page 95

How to "Ride" a Poem

Find and mark the ten spelling errors.

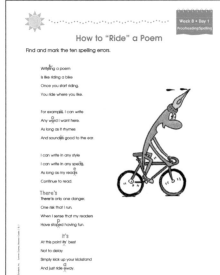

Writing a poem
Is like riding a bike
Once you start riding,
You ride where you like.

For exampil, I can write
Any wyrd I want here.
As long as it rhymes
And sounds good to the ear.

I can write in any style
I can write in any speds,
As long as my readrs
Continue to read.

There's
There's only one danger.
One risk that I run,
When I sense that my readers
Have stoped having fun.

It's
At this point its best
Not to delay
Simply kick up your kickstand
And just ride away.

95

page 96

One, or More

A **singular noun** names one person, place, or thing. A **plural noun** names more than one person, place, or thing. Add **-s** to form the plural of most nouns.

A. Each sentence has an underlined noun. On the line, write S if it is a singular noun. Write P if it is a plural noun.

1. She has a new <u>baby</u>. — S

2. <u>It</u> is very cute. — S

3. She has small <u>fingers</u>. — P

4. She drinks from a <u>bottle</u>. — S

5. I can tell my <u>friends</u> all about it. — P

B. Read each sentence. Underline the singular noun. Circle the plural noun.

1. The baby has two sisters.

2. The nightgown has pockets.

3. Her hand has tiny fingers.

4. My parents have a baby.

5. The father has three girls.

C. Complete the chart. Write the singular or plural of each noun.

Singular	Plural
fence	fences
train	trains
gate	gates
cow	cows

96

page 97

The Milky Way

The **main idea** of a story tells what the story is mostly about. **Details** in a story tell more information about the main idea.

What do you think of when you hear the words, "Milky Way?" Do you think of a candy bar? Well, there is another Milky Way, and you live in it! It is our galaxy. A galaxy is a grouping of stars. Scientists have learned that there are many galaxies in outer space. The Milky Way is a spiral-shaped galaxy with swirls of stars spinning out from the center of it. Scientists believe there are about 200 billion stars in the Milky Way. In our solar system, many planets orbit the sun. One of them is Earth. Even from Earth, on a clear night away from city lights, you can see part of the Milky Way. It is called that because so many stars close together look like a milky white stripe across the sky. However, if you looked at it with a telescope, you would see that it is made up of thousands of stars.

Complete the main idea and each detail about the story.

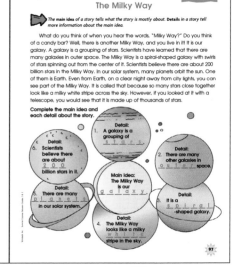

Detail:
1. A galaxy is a grouping of <u>s t a r s</u>.

Detail:
6. Scientists believe there are about <u>2 0 0</u> billion stars in it.

Detail:
2. There are many other galaxies in <u>o u t e r</u> space.

Main Idea:
The Milky Way is our <u>g a l a x y</u>.

Detail:
5. There are many <u>p l a n e t s</u> in our solar system.

Detail:
3. It is a <u>s p i r a l</u> -shaped galaxy.

Detail:
4. The Milky Way looks like a milky <u>s t r i p e</u> stripe in the sky.

97

Puzzle It Out!

Use the words in the Word Box to complete the sentences below.
Then write the words in the correct spaces in the puzzle.

Across

1. My name was the first _____word_____ that I learned to spell.

3. Sam washed the dishes so they were sparkling _____clean_____.

4. The weather today is _____warm_____ but not hot.

5. At the end of second grade, our teacher said we were _____ready_____ for third.

Down

2. Will you share my popcorn, or do you want your _____own_____?

3. She has to _____carry_____ the baby because he's too little to walk.

6. We had burgers for dinner last night, and we're having them _____again_____ tonight.

Word Box

carry   warm
own   clean
again   word
ready

page 98

More Fun With Fractions

A fraction has two numbers. The top number tells the parts of the whole.
The bottom number tells how many total parts there are.

A. $\frac{10}{10}$ is the whole circle.

Color $\frac{8}{10}$ of the circle.

How much is not colored? $\frac{2}{10}$

B. $\frac{10}{10}$ is the whole rectangle.

Color $\frac{4}{10}$ of the rectangle.

How much is not colored? $\frac{6}{10}$

$\frac{10}{10} - \frac{8}{10} = \frac{2}{10}$

$\frac{10}{10} - \frac{4}{10} = \frac{6}{10}$

C. Solve this fraction equation. Cross out the dogs to help you.

$\frac{10}{10} - \frac{3}{10} = \frac{7}{10}$

page 99

Exclamations and Commands

An **exclamation** is a sentence that shows strong feeling.
A **command** is a sentence that gives an order.

A. Read each sentence. Write E on the line if the sentence is an exclamation. Write C if the sentence is a command.

1. They chase buffaloes!   E
2. You have to go, too.   C
3. Wait at the airport.   C
4. It snows all the time!   E
5. Alligators live in the sewers!   E
6. Look at the horse.   C
7. That's a great-looking horse!   E
8. Write a letter to Seymour.   C

B. Complete each exclamation and command.

1. I feel _____!
2. Help your _____
3. That's a _____
4. I lost _____ Answers will vary. _____!
5. Turn the _____
6. Come watch the _____
7. Please let me _____

page 100

Lulu to the Rescue

VOLUME X   Anyplace, USA   **Monday, June 11**

JoAnne Altsman always thought her pet pig LuLu was a good companion. Now she also thinks of LuLu as a hero. Why? When JoAnne suffered a heart attack in 1998, LuLu saved her life. JoAnne was vacationing in her camper when she fell ill. She yelled for help, but no one heard her cries. LuLu knew that JoAnne was in trouble. She pushed through a dog door and ran to the road. She tried to stop passing cars but had no luck. LuLu hurried back to the camper three times to see how JoAnne was.

At last LuLu did something drivers were sure to notice. She lay down on the road and stuck her feet in the air. Finally, a car stopped. The driver got out and followed LuLu back to the camper. JoAnne heard the man knocking on the door. "There's something wrong with your pig!" he yelled.

"There's something wrong with me!" JoAnne yelled back. "Call 911!"

Before long, help was on its way. Today JoAnne is well, and she's grateful for her pet pig. Without LuLu, she would have died.

1. Where was JoAnne when she fell ill?
   A. on vacation
   B. at school
   C. in her home
   D. at work

2. Why did LuLu push her way out of the camper and run to the road?
   To get help for JoAnne

3. "LuLu was a good companion." What is a companion?
   F. guard
   G. nurse
   H. doctor
   J. friend

4. What probably happened after the man knocked on the door of the camper? Tell two things that probably happened.
   Answers will vary.

page 101

Stories of Nature

Sentences should be written in the correct order to tell a story.

Finish the stories by writing a sentence about each of the last two pictures.

1.   2.   3.

First: Two birds build a nest.

Next: _____ Answers will vary. _____

Last: _____

1.   2.   3.

First: A flower bud grows.

Next: _____ Answers will vary. _____

Last: _____

page 102

Time to Group

The multiplication symbol (x) can be thought of as meaning "groups of."

3 "groups of" 4 equals 12.   5 "groups of" 2 equals 10.
$3 \times 4 = 12$ $5 \times 2 = 10$

Write the multiplication sentence for each diagram.

A. $2 \times 4 = 8$ B. $3 \times 3 = 9$ C. $3 \times 5 = 15$ D. $4 \times 3 = 12$

E. $4 \times 1 = 4$ F. $6 \times 3 = 18$ G. $8 \times 2 = 16$ H. $6 \times 4 = 24$

I. $2 \times 6 = 12$ J. $8 \times 3 = 24$ K. $3 \times 6 = 18$ L. $4 \times 5 = 2$

M. $2 \times 2 = 4$ N. $6 \times 1 = 6$ O. $5 \times 4 = 20$ P. $7 \times 2 = 14$

William has five bags of hamburgers. There are seven hamburgers in each bag. On another sheet of paper, draw pictures to show the total number of hamburgers.
Check diagram. 35 hamburgers

page 103

The Sky's the Limit

Some sentences include a list. A comma (,) is used to separate each item in the list.
For example: Mrs. Jones asked the class to work on pages two, three, and four.

Fill in the blanks to make a list in each sentence. Watch for commas!

1. I ate _____, _____,
   and _____ for breakfast.

2. We stayed with Grandma on _____,
   _____, and _____ nights.

3. I found _____ Sentences will vary. _____,
   and _____ in my party bag.

4. The boys played _____,
   _____, and
   _____ at summer camp.

5. The _____,
   and _____ ate the corn we scattered.

6. The pigs built their houses using _____,
   _____, and _____

Cut a balloon shape out of paper. On one side, list three objects that fly. On the other side, write a sentence that lists the objects shown on the right side of this page.

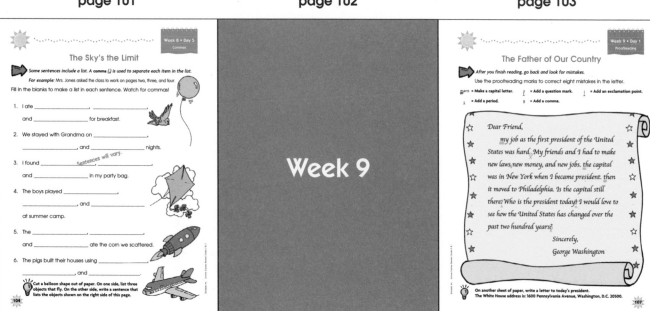

page 104

Week 9

The Father of Our Country

After you finish reading, go back and look for mistakes.
Use the proofreading marks to correct eight mistakes in the letter.

= Make a capital letter.   ? = Add a question mark.   ! = Add an exclamation point.
. = Add a period.   , = Add a comma.

Dear Friend,
my job as the first president of the United States was hard. My friends and I had to make new laws, new money, and new jobs. the capital was in New York when I became president. then it moved to Philadelphia. Is the capital still there? Who is the president today? I would love to see how the United States has changed over the past two hundred years?
Sincerely,
George Washington

On another sheet of paper, write a letter to today's president.
The White House address is: 1600 Pennsylvania Avenue, Washington, D.C. 20500.

page 107

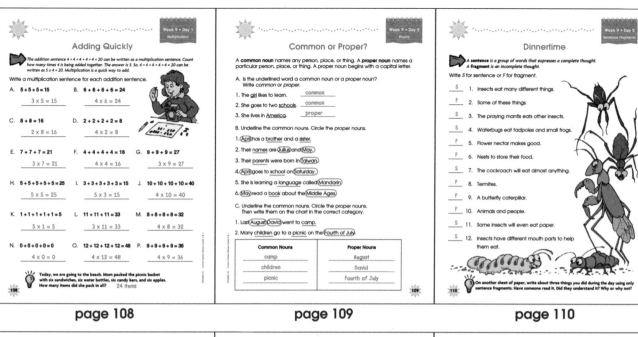

page 108

Adding Quickly

The addition sentence 4 + 4 + 4 + 4 + 4 = 20 can be written as a multiplication sentence. Count how many times 4 is being added together. The answer is 5. So, 4 + 4 + 4 + 4 + 4 = 20 can be written as 5 x 4 = 20. Multiplication is a quick way to add.

Write a multiplication sentence for each addition sentence.

A. 5 + 5 + 5 = 15
3 x 5 = 15

B. 6 + 6 + 6 + 6 = 24
4 x 6 = 24

C. 8 + 8 = 16
2 x 8 = 16

D. 2 + 2 + 2 + 2 = 8
4 x 2 = 8

E. 7 + 7 + 7 = 21
3 x 7 = 21

F. 4 + 4 + 4 + 4 = 16
4 x 4 = 16

G. 9 + 9 + 9 = 27
3 x 9 = 27

H. 5 + 5 + 5 + 5 + 5 = 25
5 x 5 = 25

I. 3 + 3 + 3 + 3 + 3 = 15
5 x 3 = 15

J. 10 + 10 + 10 + 10 = 40
4 x 10 = 40

K. 1 + 1 + 1 + 1 + 1 = 5
5 x 1 = 5

L. 11 + 11 + 11 = 33
3 x 11 = 33

M. 8 + 8 + 8 + 8 = 32
4 x 8 = 32

N. 0 + 0 + 0 + 0 = 0
4 x 0 = 0

O. 12 + 12 + 12 + 12 = 48
4 x 12 = 48

P. 9 + 9 + 9 + 9 = 36
4 x 9 = 36

Today, we are going to the beach. Mom packed the picnic basket with six sandwiches, six water bottles, six candy bars, and six apples. How many items did she pack in all? 24 items

108

page 109

Common or Proper?

A **common noun** names any person, place, or thing. A **proper noun** names a particular person, place, or thing. A proper noun begins with a capital letter.

A. Is the underlined word a common noun or a proper noun? Write *common* or *proper*.
1. The girl likes to learn. ___common___
2. She goes to two schools. ___common___
3. She lives in America. ___proper___

B. Underline the common nouns. Circle the proper nouns.
1. April has a brother and a sister.
2. Their names are Julius and May.
3. Their parents were born in Taiwan.
4. April goes to school on Saturday.
5. She is learning a language called Mandarin.
6. May read a book about the Middle Ages.

C. Underline the common nouns. Circle the proper nouns. Then write them on the chart in the correct category.
1. Last August David went to camp.
2. Many children go to a picnic on the Fourth of July.

Common Nouns	Proper Nouns
camp	August
children	David
picnic	Fourth of July

109

page 110

Dinnertime

A **sentence** is a group of words that expresses a complete thought. A **fragment** is an incomplete thought.

Write *S* for sentence or *F* for fragment.

___S___ 1. Insects eat many different things.
___F___ 2. Some of these things.
___S___ 3. The praying mantis eats other insects.
___S___ 4. Waterbugs eat tadpoles and small frogs.
___F___ 5. Flower nectar makes good.
___F___ 6. Nests to store their food.
___S___ 7. The cockroach will eat almost anything.
___F___ 8. Termites.
___F___ 9. A butterfly caterpillar.
___F___ 10. Animals and people.
___S___ 11. Some insects will even eat paper.
___S___ 12. Insects have different mouth parts to help them eat.

On another sheet of paper, write about three things you did during the day using only sentence fragments. Have someone read it. Did they understand it? Why or why not?

110

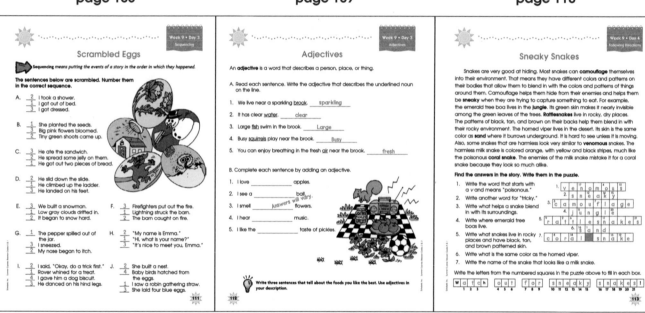

page 111

Scrambled Eggs

Sequencing means putting the events of a story in the order in which they happened.

The sentences below are scrambled. Number them in the correct sequence.

A. 2 I took a shower.
1 I got out of bed.
3 I got dressed.

B. 2 She planted the seeds.
3 Big pink flowers bloomed.
1 Tiny green shoots came up.

C. 3 He ate the sandwich.
2 He spread some jelly on them.
1 He got out two pieces of bread.

D. 2 He slid down the slide.
1 He climbed up the ladder.
3 He landed on his feet.

E. 3 We built a snowman.
2 Low gray clouds drifted in.
1 It began to snow hard.

F. 2 Firefighters put out the fire.
3 Lightning struck the barn.
1 The barn caught on fire.

G. 1 The pepper spilled out of the jar.
3 I sneezed.
2 My nose began to itch.

H. 2 "My name is Emma."
1 "Hi, what is your name?"
3 "It's nice to meet you, Emma."

I. 1 I said, "Okay, do a trick first."
2 Rover whined for a treat.
4 I gave him a dog biscuit.
3 He danced on his hind legs.

J. 3 She built a nest.
4 Baby birds hatched from the eggs.
1 I saw a robin gathering straw.
2 She laid four blue eggs.

111

page 112

Adjectives

An **adjective** is a word that describes a person, place, or thing.

A. Read each sentence. Write the adjective that describes the underlined noun on the line.
1. We live near a sparkling brook. ___sparkling___
2. It has clear water. ___clear___
3. Large fish swim in the brook. ___Large___
4. Busy squirrels play near the brook. ___Busy___
5. You can enjoy breathing in the fresh air near the brook. ___fresh___

B. Complete each sentence by adding an adjective.
1. I love _____ apples.
2. I see a _____ ball.
3. I smell _____ flowers. *Answers will vary.*
4. I hear _____ music.
5. I like the _____ taste of pickles.

Write three sentences that tell about the foods you like the best. Use adjectives in your description.

112

page 113

Sneaky Snakes

Snakes are very good at hiding. Most snakes can **camouflage** themselves into their environment. That means they have different colors and patterns on their bodies that allow them to blend in with the colors and patterns of things around them. Camouflage helps them hide from their enemies and helps them be **sneaky** when they are trying to capture something to eat. For example, the emerald tree boa lives in the **jungle**. Its green skin makes it nearly invisible among the green leaves of the trees. **Rattlesnakes** live in rocky, dry places. The patterns of black, tan, and brown on their backs help them blend in with their rocky environment. The horned viper lives in the desert. Its skin is the same color as **sand** where it burrows underground. It is hard to see unless it is moving. Also, some snakes that are harmless look very similar to **venomous** snakes. The harmless milk snake is colored orange, with yellow and black stripes, much like the poisonous **coral** snake. The enemies of the milk snake mistake it for a coral snake because they look so much alike.

Find the answers in the story. Write them in the puzzle.
1. Write the word that starts with a *v* and means "poisonous."
2. Write another word for "tricky."
3. Write what helps a snake blend in with its surroundings.
4. Write where emerald tree boas live.
5. Write what snakes live in rocky places and have black, tan, and brown patterned skin.
6. Write what is the same color as the horned viper.
7. Write the name of the snake that looks like a milk snake.

Across/down puzzle answers:
1. venomous
2. sneaky
3. camouflage
4. jungle
5. rattlesnakes
6. sand
7. coral snake

Write the letters from the numbered squares in the puzzle above to fill in each box.
W a t c h   o u t   f o r   s n e a k y   s n a k e s !

113

page 114

How It Is

Circle the word that best completes each sentence and write it on the line.

1. An ant is black, and a grasshopper is ___green___
A. blue B. fuzzy C. green

2. A shirt is cotton, and a jar is ___glass___
A. glass B. silk C. jam

3. A hill is rolling, and a river is ___winding___
A. winding B. rainy C. steep

4. A daisy is white, and a rose is ___red___
A. green B. dirty C. red

5. A ring is round, and a box is ___square___
A. wool B. square C. happy

6. An elephant is large, and a mouse is ___small___
A. small B. huge C. yellow

7. A puddle is muddy, and a pool is ___clear___
A. sad B. clear C. shy

8. A hammer is hard, and a pillow is ___soft___
A. sleepy B. sharp C. soft

Discuss with someone why you did not choose the other words.

114

page 115

"Fun and Games"

Some words like "hammer and nails" and "salt and pepper" just go together.

Choose a word from the box to

sooner	right
chips	sweet
order	lost
sugar	effect
bacon	fun
shine	business
error	easy
name	gentlemen
cup	alive
cents	pots

1. cause and ___effect___
2. ___fun___ and games
3. ___cup___ and saucer
4. cream and ___sugar___
5. ___lost___ and found
6. ___name___ and address
7. ladies and ___gentlemen___
8. law and ___order___
9. ___sweet___ and sour
10. nice and ___easy___
11. trial and ___error___
12. ___pots___ and pans
13. fish and ___chips___
14. rain or ___shine___
15. ___business___ or pleasure
16. ___right___ or wrong
17. dead or ___alive___
18. dollars and ___cents___
19. ___bacon___ and eggs
20. ___sooner___ or later

On another sheet of paper, list three other pairs of words that go together.

115

page 116

Great Graphing

A. How many pennies equal 5¢? How many nickels equal 5¢? Color in the boxes on the graph to show your answers.

	1	2	3	4	5	6	7	8	9	10
Pennies										
Nickels										

B. How many pennies equal 10¢? How many nickels equal 10¢? How many dimes equal 10¢? Color in the boxes on the graph to show your answers.

	1	2	3	4	5	6	7	8	9	10
Pennies										
Nickels										
Dimes										

C. How many pennies equal 25¢? How many nickels equal 25¢? How many quarters equal 25¢? Color in the boxes on the graph to show your answers.

	1	2	3	4	5	6	7	8	9	10	11	12	13	14	15	16	17	18	19	20	21	22	23	24	25
Pennies																									
Nickels																									
Quarters																									

116

page 119

page 120

page 121

page 122

page 123

page 124

page 125

page 126

Where the Sun Shines

Florida is known for its pleasant weather. In fact, it has earned the nickname "Sunshine State." As a result of its warm, sunny climate, Florida is a good place for growing fruits, such as oranges and grapefruits. Many older people go to live in Florida. They enjoy the good weather. Northerners on vacation also visit Florida for the same reason.

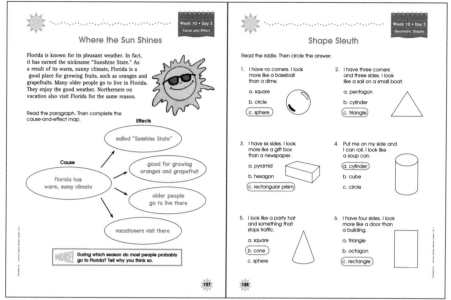

Read the paragraph. Then complete the cause-and-effect map.

Effects

Cause

Florida has warm, sunny climate

called "Sunshine State"

good for growing oranges and grapefruit

older people go to live there

vacationers visit there

MORE! During which season do most people probably go to Florida? Tell why you think so.

127

Shape Sleuth

Read the riddle. Then circle the answer.

1. I have no corners. I look more like a baseball than a dime.
   a. square
   b. circle
   c. sphere

2. I have three corners and three sides. I look like a sail on a small boat.
   a. pentagon
   b. cylinder
   c. triangle

3. I have six sides. I look more like a gift box than a newspaper.
   a. pyramid
   b. hexagon
   c. rectangular prism

4. Put me on my side and I can roll. I look like a soup can.
   a. cylinder
   b. cube
   c. circle

5. I look like a party hat and something that stops traffic.
   a. square
   b. cone
   c. sphere

6. I have four sides. I look more like a door than a building.
   a. triangle
   b. octagon
   c. rectangle

128

THIS CERTIFIES THAT

_____

IS NOW READY

FOR GRADE _____

CONGRATULATIONS!

_____

I'm proud of you!